Transgenerational Healing of Oedipus at Colonus

BY THE SAME AUTHOR

With many illustrations the author shows how analyzing our ancestors' lives helps us to understand problematic conditions and heals all kinds of symptoms. Goethe already explained: *What we have received from our ancestors, we must assimilate until it becomes a part of ourselves if we want it to be an enrichment instead of a burden*.

This is the first time an author has merged contemporary transgenerational therapy and universal wisdoms. In his book, he also reveals how modern practices can benefit from mythological teachings, in line with the ancient maxim: *Know Thyself*.

The Ancients already knew the therapeutic potential of the family links between generations that we rediscover in modern transgenerational practices. Far from being a new fashion, the recognition of transgenerational processes dates back to the first shamanic type of communities. Their methods to cure "The Ancestor Syndrome" offer to contemporary therapies essential historical references and valuable teachings.

With the contribution of specialists from different backgrounds, this collective book presents a wide spectrum of perspectives to bridge traditional and modern knowledges.

Tony T. Gaillard

Transgenerational Healing of Oedipus at Colonus

Unveiling a Universal Therapeutic Model

Genesis Editions

By the same author,

- ***Transgenerational Therapy***, *Healing the Inherited Burden*, 2020.
- ***Shamanism, Ancestors and Transgenerational Therapy***, (collective book), 2020.

And in French :

- ***Intégrer ses héritages transgénérationnels***, 2018.
- ***L'intégration transgénérationnelle***, *ces histoires qui hantent le présent*, 2018.
- ***A propos de la métamorphose d'Œdipe en héros de Colone***, 2014.
- ***L'autre Œdipe***, *De Freud à Sophocle*, 2013.
- ***Sophocle thérapeute***, *La guérison d'Œdipe à Colone*, 2013.

Author's website: www.en.t-gaillard.com

Cover page: **Hebe**, goddess of immortality, serving nectar and ambrosia to the gods.

Original French title:
"A propos de la métamorphose d'Œdipe en héros de Colone"

GENESIS Editions
18, rue De-Candolle, 1205 Geneva, Switzerland

www.genesis-editions.com/en

Distribution: INGRAM

2020, First Edition.

ISBN: 978-2-940540-35-8

Contents

Foreword 7

Preface: Summaries of *Oedipus the King* and *Oedipus at Colonus* 9

Introduction 15

I From Thebes to Colonus 29

II A Transgenerational Curse 45

III The Legacy of Laius 53

IV The Legacy of Jocasta 65

V From Cadmus to Oedipus 75

VI Oedipus Makes Amends for Family Debts 103

VII Oedipus reconnects to the Origins 111

Conclusion 131

Glossary 143

Bibliography 167

Foreword

This book, intended for a mixed audience, summarizes my extensive research on the myth of Oedipus, the results of which have shaken up the most common ideas about Sophocles' masterpieces. These discoveries reveal and challenge some of the modern prejudices about how we relate to our origins and, more generally, our relationship to the world that gave birth to us.

By associating traditional practice and contemporary transgenerational therapy, my analysis reveals unexpected teachings that lies concealed in Sophocles' work on Oedipus. Among the most important of these are the metamorphosis of Oedipus, a theme which is present in many ancient traditions, but which has been largely forgotten by our civilization. For more than two millennia this aspect of Sophocles' work has never truly been given the recognition it deserves. It is only thanks to the emergence of contemporary transgenerational therapies that we can understand the importance of the family curse that affected Oedipus at birth and thus reconnect with the profound meaning of the story.

The analysis of family transgenerational legacies, and the related principles underlying Oedipus' plays, thus restores the role of Sophocles and other tragedians of his time, in guiding the collective consciousness and mediating between the visible and invisible worlds. For centuries before the Christian era the tragedians of Athens fulfilled an essential function for the community, synthesizing religion, art, knowledge, and its transmission. Sophocles' message remains as relevant today as it was in his time. When we understand his symbolic dimension, Sophocles' teaching provides answers full of wisdom for modern existential questions. His plays incorporate knowledge about the causes of many current issues: infertile couples, antagonism between believers and atheists, limits of rational thinking, sadistic abuse and instrumentalization of written laws, the culture of a false Self, the remoteness of the unwritten laws of life, the relationship with nature (ecology) and with the Other (humanization), sexual differences, self-knowledge and the consequences of loss of love for truth itself (*Aletheia* in Greek).

This new understanding of the myth of Oedipus functions as a key which enables us to bring together the two worlds of ancient and contemporary knowledge. Because they shed light upon realities which have been too long concealed, the results of such a discovery are numerous and promising. In this perspective, the transgenerational analysis of the Oedipus myth and the discovery of its true meaning offers us a formidable opportunity to take up some modern prejudices that have until now remained unnoticed, namely the modern politic to cut ourselves form where we come, as if we would not belong to the world which gave us life.

This book has been freed as much as possible from theoretical or therapeutic considerations. The most in-depth theoretical exposition of transgenerational phenomena, with many therapeutic study cases, was reserved for another essay, translated as *Transgenerational Integration: Healing the Inherited Burden.*

I would like to acknowledge my gratitude to Nancy M. Hoffman, Ph.D., my longtime friend and colleague in New York City for her time and attention to this edition.

Tony Thierry Gaillard, May 2020.

Preface

Summary of *Oedipus the King*

While Oedipus is King of Thebes, his subjects gather outside the palace to ask for his help. An epidemic of the plague is decimating the kingdom and rendering the crops, the livestock and the men and women of the city infertile. Oedipus replies that he too is troubled by these circumstances and that he is determined to heal his kingdom. He has already sent Creon, the brother of his wife Jocasta, to consult the oracle about the problem.

Upon his return, Creon repeats what the oracle has told him: namely that the plague has been caused by the unsolved murder of the former King of Thebes, Laius. Oedipus therefore commits to unearthing the whole truth about this event; he decides to investigate and to find and punish the guilty party. He summons Tiresias the seer who, though blind, nonetheless possesses the faculty of clairvoyance. At first the seer refuses to tell Oedipus what he knows, because it could provoke another tragedy. Angered, Oedipus threatens Tiresias and forces him to speak. Against his will, Tiresias gives in and reveals that Oedipus himself is the guilty man for whom he is searching. He explains that the guilty party is both the brother and the father of his own children, the son and the husband of the woman who brought him into the world.

Oedipus is far from being able to take in such a revelation and instead suspects that Tiresias and Creon are conspiring to usurp his throne. Jocasta tries to calm the rising conflict by minimizing Tiresias's words: "No one is capable of correctly interpreting the oracles without the risk of making a mistake." The proof, she adds, is the prophecy announcing that Laius would die at the hands of his son, whereas Laius was killed by highwaymen at the crossing of the roads to Delphi and Daulie, according to the testimony of a servant who escaped.

However, Jocasta's arguments fail to calm Oedipus. He remembers an old story that circulated when a drunken man at a festival declared that Oedipus was a foundling. This announcement surprised Oedipus, who had always been considered and treated as the son of Polybius and Merope, the king and queen of Corinth. And although they deny the allegations, Oedipus is so anguished, so haunted by nightmares that he himself goes to consult the oracle. Instead of replying, the oracle predicts that he will marry his mother, bring a curse upon his descendants, and kill his father. Overwhelmed, Oedipus takes off in the direction of Thebes, instead of returning to Corinth and those whom he considers his parents, to avoid the fulfillment of this tragic destiny. Along the way, a man starts a fight with him about who has the right of way at a crossroads. In the ensuing struggle, Oedipus kills the aggressor and several members of his entourage, except for one servant who escapes.

To bring this affair to light, Oedipus gives the order to find the escaped servant who saw the highwaymen that killed Laius. Then suddenly, a messenger from Corinth arrives and announces that king Polybius has died from illness and old age. This news comforts Oedipus, who believes that he has thereby escaped the prophecy: he has not and cannot now kill his father. Then the messenger explains that this concern is misplaced since Polybius is not Oedipus' biological father. The messenger himself received the infant Oedipus from the hands of a shepherd of the house of Laius whom he met on the slopes of Mount Cithaeron. Instead of abandoning the baby to the beasts of the fields, hanging him by his feet as King Laius had commanded, the shepherd took pity on the child and gave him to a foreigner. When the new-born child was taken to Corinth, Polybius and Merope, who suffered from infertility, decided to adopt him and gave him the name Oedipus on account of his swollen feet.

In the face of these revelations, Jocasta is troubled and asks Oedipus not to continue his investigation. But Oedipus is determined to learn the truth. Since he was born at Thebes, he wants to know the identity of his parents, in the hope of finding out whether or not he is of noble blood. Otherwise, what could explain why Jocasta has asked him to stop the investigation unless she is ashamed of the possibility that his origins are humble? Oedipus intends to follow through with the investigation. Convinced that he is, in any event, a "son of good Fortune", he has no sense of shame about it.

Next, however, they bring in the servant who claimed that Laius was assassinated by highwaymen. Straightaway, the messenger from Corinth recognizes the servant as the man he met on Mount Cithaeron, the very man who entrusted Oedipus to him. Forced to speak, the old servant admits that this infant was none other than the son of Laius and Jocasta, who had condemned the child to death on Mount Cithaeron because of the prophecy which declared that Oedipus would kill his parents. However, the servant was not able to bring himself to obey Laius' order and decided to entrust the infant to the messenger who came from Corinth.

When he discovers his true history, Oedipus realizes that despite himself he has indeed committed patricide and incest as the oracle predicted. Already in a state of shock over this revelation, he then receives word that Jocasta has just hanged herself in her room. Oedipus rushes there, and in a fit of suffering, he stabs out his eyes with the brooches securing the robes of the woman who was both his mother and his wife.

In his state of turmoil, Oedipus demands to be sent into exile and abandoned to his accursed fate. However, Creon decides to consult the oracle to learn what should be done.

Summary of Oedipus at Colonus

Accompanied by his eldest daughter, Antigone, Oedipus arrives at Colonus, fatigued from his journey in exile. He has barely had a chance to sit down when a native of the region asks him to leave the area because it is a sacred place, where the presence of human beings is forbidden. This announcement brings joy to Oedipus because it means that he has finally arrived at the end of his painful exile. He confides to his daughter that the oracle also predicted that he would find hospitality in this sacred place where the Eumenides (or Furies) live and that if he settled there, he would become a benefactor to those who welcomed him.

Oedipus asks that they inform the king of this country, Theseus, that he could profit greatly in exchange for a small favour. While waiting for Theseus to arrive, the wise men of Colonus spend their time trying to get rid of Oedipus to avoid his desecrating the sacred place with his presence. It is then that the second daughter of Oedipus, Ismene, arrives unexpectedly. She announces that war is imminent between her two brothers, Polynices and Eteocles, who are both laying claim to the throne of Thebes. She adds that the Thebans will try to capture Oedipus on account of a new oracle predicting that fate will be kind to those who have hold of him or his mortal remains. Ismene goes on to explain that although the Thebans are trying to seize him in order to avoid the worst of fates, this does not mean that they will let him return to the land of his birth. They plan on just holding him near the border. Forewarned as to the true intentions of the Thebans, Oedipus curses his sons who, once again, value the crown of Thebes more than their father's well-being. (When he asked to be sent into exile, they refused. Later, when Oedipus' suffering had ceased, and he would have preferred a different fate, they again refuse to defend him when he was condemned to exile).

Then Theseus arrives to meet with Oedipus. After they exchange a few words of mutual respect, Theseus declares that he knows well what it means to live in exile, having experienced it for himself; as a simple mortal man, he is no more able to control the future than Oedipus. Therefore, he grants Oedipus' request for hospitality and promises to protect him. Relieved, Oedipus promises that, before he dies, he will entrust Theseus with a secret that will ensure that his people shall never be in need.

At this point, Creon makes an appearance and proposes that Oedipus should follow him back to Thebes. However, thanks to the warning from Ismene, Oedipus refuses to be duped. He accuses Creon of trying to deceive him with his use of fine language. Creon drops the masquerade. He announces that he has already kidnapped Ismene and then orders his guards to kidnap Antigone, not without provoking a storm of protest from the natives of Colonus. Carried away by his anger, Creon threatens to seize Oedipus himself. He justifies this by accusing Oedipus of being a criminal. Oedipus replies that he is innocent of the crimes of which he is accused, that he is the victim of what the gods decided for him before he was even born. And as to being reproached for having married Jocasta, Oedipus admits that it was an illegal marriage, but explains that he was innocent because he knew nothing about the circumstances of his birth. Going on the offensive, he then attacks Creon for having no conscience, by reminding him of the causes of his suffering and continuing to persecute him despite his innocence. After witnessing this confrontation, faithful to his promise, Theseus engages in battle with the kidnappers and returns the daughters to Oedipus.

Polynices then asks to meet with his father. He begs Oedipus to help him in his fight against his brother for possession of the throne of Thebes. Then Oedipus explains that he is no longer the same person that he was, and that his sons are no longer his sons. He would not know how to relieve the curse that weighs upon them nor deflect a destiny they have brought upon themselves.

At this point a great crash is heard: it is the thunderbolt of Zeus, calling Oedipus to his final meeting place. Oedipus sends for Theseus to accompany him in the last episode of his life. Oedipus repeats to his host that he is going to bequeath to him a secret that will guarantee his prosperity. However, he insists that in order to enjoy such happiness, he must never forget the name of Oedipus.

A messenger who accompanied the two men from afar reports to Ismene and Antigone the spectacle that he has witnessed. The thunderbolt of Zeus summoned Oedipus while Theseus covered his eyes as if dazzled by the divine presence. Oedipus will die mysteriously, either raised by the gods or engulfed by the earth. Be that as it may, when Theseus returns to Antigone and Ismene, he announces that they can stop lamenting because they now benefit from the protection of the dead. Before dying, Oedipus has thus kept his promise and delivered to Theseus the secret that will guarantee the prosperity of his kingdom.

Become such as you are,
having learned what that is.
Pindar

Introduction

The myth of Oedipus hides ageless teachings that have not yet been recognized. More than ever, this wisdom can help us to make sense of today's world. It sheds light on ourselves and our lives and invites us to better understand our interactions with multiple realities, whether conscious or unconscious, visible or invisible.

Reclaiming this ancient knowledge also means reconnecting with our own roots, especially their symbolic and atemporal forms, which link us to the very sources of life, here and now. This is a path that takes us beyond the limits of consciousness and brings us closer to our true Selves. Like riding the mythical winged horse, Pegasus, for this journey we will have to learn the symbolic language of myth to speak with gods and ancestors, and thus access our unconscious dimensions, whether in the light of day or in the darkness of night.

As advocated by the ancient Greeks, knowing about our true Self and learning the symbolic language of the myths helps us to dialogue with our deepest strata, our shadows. Myths can introduce us to this greater reality, especially the story of Oedipus.

Deciphering a myth and solving the enigma it conceals is an exercise that has the value of an introduction into this dimension of truth which escapes us most of the time—the knowledge of our true Self. When he discovers the secret of his adoption, Oedipus wonders: "Who am I?" Let there be no mistake: his questioning is not just about social or family identity. Above all, it denounces our pretense, our beliefs and our illusions, to question the meaning of our lives and free us from our collective and individual alienations.

Regarding this perspective, specific to the time of Sophocles, we must recognize that the innumerable modern interpretations of the Oedipus myth have raised new questions rather than providing the necessary answers. Modern ears have remained deaf to the genuine teachings hidden in Sophocles' work. The reason for such an impasse may well come from our disregard of inherited curses and debts between the generations and our blindness to what is going on there. This is, in any case, the thesis that I will defend in the following pages: to discover the true meaning of the myth, we must first reclaim the old consciousness of the possible tragic consequences of transgenerational legacy. In Sophocles' time, in any case, it was understood that the transgressions and failings of the ancestors were likely to be perpetuated over several generations, like a family curse. Even with specific reference to Oedipus and his family, this aspect of Sophocles' work has never really been considered.

Although they are dotted throughout Sophocles' text, the references to these transgenerational legacies have so far not received the attention they deserve. The modern unawareness of the links between the generations, as if one should not give too much credence to these old and "ridiculous beliefs", merits questioning. As a result of this loss, we no longer understand important passages in Sophocles' text, even the most explicit. Who today would claim to know perfectly the workings of these unwritten transgenerational laws which Oedipus refers to when he addresses Creon? "All this I suffered; I did not want it. Such was the pleasure of the gods; no doubt they were pursuing my family with an ancient curse [...] If an oracle had predicted to my father that he would die by the hand of his children, by what means, tell me, could you blame me, since my father, at that time had not yet fathered me, since my mother had not yet given birth to me, since I had not yet been conceived!"

To grasp Oedipus' argument, one must already know that, for the ancient Greeks, this "hatred by the gods" is akin to a curse on a family line because of a transgression committed by an ancestor. If not remedied or amended, the debt persists and affects the fate of his descendants. This curse, or *ate*[1], strikes all members of the same lineage, linked to the past event by blood ties. In a culture where the members of a family form the same unit (before the development of the modern notion of supposedly independent individuality), it was natural to question the share of ancestors' responsibility for the fate of descendants.

Thus, in the case of the Labdacids, Oedipus' family, it was important to discover the person responsible for the tragic fate of Oedipus. Who was the ancestor behind this

---

[1] In Greek mythology *Atë* is known as the goddess of evil, misfortune, obsession, guilt and mischief. She was known to lure men into actions that would usually end in their demise.

curse, and what actions did he commit which should be cleared in order to remedy it? Since he was not even born, it couldn't be Oedipus! In any case, this is the argument that he puts forward and that hits the bull's eye at a time when everyone knew and feared the terrible consequences of such transgenerational legacies.

How could we judge the work of Sophocles without first grasping the meaning of the words which he puts into Oedipus' mouth, without piercing the nature of these transgenerational curses, or first reclaiming their ancient consciousness?

Even if some of the great authors still pay attention to what is replayed within the same family line, we are a long way from suspecting the extent of this phenomenon. After more than two thousand years of repression of traditional knowledge, not much remains. With the change of civilization in Athens, and the denigration of the ancient knowledge which accompanied it, the importance of what is transmitted between the generations has gradually escaped us. Recently, the philosopher Peter Sloterdijk has analyzed how modernity has developed on the oblivion of genealogical links by reversing temporality: "One would rather believe that heredity as such now appears as a defect against which the moderns rebel every time they reach a point of resistance. They increasingly reject the old dowry that oppresses them - whether it be slavery due to biological determinations or the impregnations of class, education, culture and family. The agents of uprooting do not like to acknowledge that such "enslavement" by origin can just as well be positive conditions for a defined, concrete and successful life. Moreover, in the modern economy of credits, this set of fatalities is reinforced by the creditors who insist on having their loans repaid, and who are as obstinate as in the past, the goddesses of vengeance using a curse. Every time the interest in disinheritance and starting from scratch is inflamed, we are on the ground of authentic modernity."[2] Thus, modern civilization is characterized by the temporal inversion of what would now make sense: "It is the ends and no longer the beginnings that would decide the meaning of the current conditions. It would be the futures that would really count, not the origins."[3]

In a traditional culture, elders were considered a gift to the community that could benefit from their experiences. Their value was much greater than that of a newborn baby who would have little to pass on to others. They are now rare these elders still considered to be the guardians of memory and knowledge, the transmitters of family history. Today, most older people will probably not necessarily have benefited from such a transmission from their own parents and are unaware of the importance of passing on their (true) life stories to their descendants. As we have forgotten the importance of transgenerational inheritance, the elderly have lost this potential for transmission and it is up to the newborn to be invested when it could be useful in their parent's race towards the future, especially if they suffer from uprooting of which they would not even be aware - neither individually nor collectively.

However, since the 1980s, therapeutic results in transgenerational analysis have been accumulating. Together with more recent research in epigenetics, we now realize how much transgenerational legacy affects the fate of

---

[2] Peter Sloterdijk (2018), *Après nous le déluge, les temps modernes comme expérience antigénéalogique*, Payot, Paris. [*After us, the deluge, modern times as an anti-genealogical experience.*]
[3] Ibidem.

individuals. This renewed awareness of the links between the generations redirects us to what the ancients already knew.

Blood Ties

Even if historians and anthropologists have stressed the importance of blood ties in traditional societies, have they understood the reasons why? Traditionally, descendants were inseparable from their ancestors and their origins, by which they were identified, for example by the names of ancestors or the land of origin. This is an essential point that we find at the beginning of *Oedipus Rex*. When he addresses his subjects, as if it were necessary to make an introduction, Oedipus does not fail to refer to their origin: "Children, offspring of ancestor Cadmus." Indeed, Cadmus is the founder of Thebes and all the Thebans are his descendants, his “new offspring".

Hellenists have also stressed the importance of blood ties. For example, they recall a controversy over the legitimacy of Pericles as head of Athens. Even though he had been the builder of Athens and of its growing influence, Pericles, contemporary of Sophocles, was blamed by some when the plague devastated Athens, from 430 to 426 BC. There were those who remembered the curse on his family, the Alcmeonids. At the time, they had been banished and ostracized, because of a transgression committed by one of their ancestors. Due to this curse, Pericles was accused of being responsible for the plague epidemics by the mere fact of his presence as head of the city—a similar situation to that of Oedipus in *Oedipus Rex,* when Tiresias explains that the king is himself responsible for the misfortunes of Thebes and the heir of a family curse. However, neither Pericles nor Oedipus can take it in. It is too unbearable for them to be confronted with this aspect of themselves, namely their unconscious and inherited shadows. But Sophocles tells us about the stages leading up to this essential revelation and the resulting metamorphosis, until everything returns to a higher order, back to prosperity, as he explains at the end of *Oedipus at Colonus*.

To incriminate the leader of a city or a country and make him bear responsibility for its misfortune is congruous with the collective consciousness of the time. This society also questions the potential consequences for the heirs of family curses and their possible acquittals. For how long was it necessary to banish the descendants of a transgressing ancestor? What would be the possible collective consequences if they were granted hospitality? How could they redeem themselves in the eyes of the city and the gods so as to be reintegrated into the community?

As we will see, Sophocles answers all these questions in his work on Oedipus. After the crisis and the wilderness of exile, Sophocles tells us about the metamorphosis of Oedipus at Colonus and his return to grace with the gods. He thus clearly shows that Oedipus has paid off the debt responsible for the curse he has unconsciously inherited.

Modern Oversight of Transgenerational Legacy

Progressively alienated from the knowledge of the ancients into which Sophocles was initiated, the new civilization developing in Athens represses the notion of transgenerational debts. Confusing religious belief with knowledge, modernity will elude and forget related problems. If it does not resolve anything, this head-in-the-sand policy reveals, above all, the increasing inability of men to understand these legacies and remedy them if necessary. Today, transgenerational analyzes remind us of the importance of these phenomena. As we will see in detail, they also provide a better understanding of the principles underlying Sophocles' work.

Our ignorance of what is passed on through generations and its consequences has led our society to believe that our origins do not really matter. This is a misunderstanding that allows for astonishing, unethical practices: sperm donation without transmission of the father's identity, the anonymity of the biological parents during abandonment, surrogate mothers, adoptions without acts defining the origins, uprooting and forced placements of children, filiation secrets, etc. In the eyes of an ancient sage, failing to respect these unwritten laws was sheer folly. Even in the case of one's worst enemies, to dehumanize a generation in this way amounted to attracting the worst curses to oneself and one's family. A Chinese proverb warns of the consequences of these practices: "To ignore one's ancestors is to be a stream without a source, a tree without roots."

What hides such carelessness from our roots, this lack of legacy of the history of our families and our societies? More than ever the question is topical. Above all, such a policy of ignorance does not exempt us from the consequences of transgenerational legacy, quite the contrary! Being oblivious of this transgenerational legacy serves to increase its alienating power for both individuals and collectively. And, as we will see from the analysis of Oedipus' fate, it is not by ignoring this legacy or because it has become unconscious that the individual escapes the consequences of transgenerational legacies.

The transgenerational analysis of Sophocles' masterpieces will refresh our memories. As if he had anticipated that modernity would forget this knowledge and as if it were necessary to preserve its memory, Sophocles leaves us a teaching in the best of all possible forms, both symbolic and artistic. Loyal to the tradition of hermeneutic teachings, his message is invisible to those who are not prepared for it, whilst it could not be more transparent to initiates. This is, moreover, one of the challenges of this transgenerational analysis of the myth: preparing readers to perceive this transgenerational reality, invisible at first glance, but which becomes obvious as we progress. Fortunately, this work is facilitated by the myth itself which leads us there as it triggers the need to discover its true meaning. Along the way, it forces our intelligence into its final entrenchments, requiring a widening of the field of possibilities.

In *Oedipus Rex*, Sophocles shows us how much the secret identity of his real parents (Laius and Jocasta) has impacted Oedipus' life. He believed his parents were Polybius and Merope, but they suffered from sterility and had adopted Oedipus who was found abandoned on Mount Cithaeron, without revealing the story to him. Under these conditions, Oedipus cannot integrate his origins, the story of his ancestor Cadmus, the founder of Thebes or that of the two lines he fathered, the Labdacids and the Spartoi and their permanent fight for the throne.

Unlike modern minds who underestimate the consequences of ignoring parentage and family history, Sophocles presents the worst possible scenario with incest and patricide. However, and it is here that we can measure the extent of his wisdom, Sophocles also teaches us how Oedipus will absolve the family debts he has inherited and, in Colonus, become the hero who will guarantee prosperity, revered and glorified by his hosts. Indeed, and we will analyze this later, once the secret of his origins is revealed, Oedipus will be able to integrate his transgenerational legacy. Thus, becoming aware of what subconsciously inhabited and alienated him appears to be the starting point for integration. To make it even clearer, Sophocles couples Oedipus' healing with the transformation of the plague in Thebes into a promise of prosperity in Colonus. In truth, the evolution of the situation reflects the consequences of a deep work of integrating one's origins, the reunion with oneself, or with the true Self, the benefit of which is reflected externally.

If Sophocles recounts Oedipus' descent into hell in the first part of his work, it is because he masters the principles of transgenerational healing and has already planned to present his hero for rebirth and transfiguration. He knows what afflicts Oedipus and Pericles and he knows what it will take to remedy it. Without a doubt, the metamorphosis of Oedipus is at the heart of Sophocles' hidden teaching.

To further emphasize this individual and collective healing perspective in Sophocles' work, we should also remember that he was descended from a family that worshiped divine healers. And most significantly, he was also a priest of Asclepius, which implies that he had been initiated into ancient wisdom. Little wonder that he learned the causes of transgenerational alienation and the way to resolve them. That is why he could afford to dramatize the worst tragedies they could cause–like that of Oedipus. Seen from this angle, his work appears as a major teaching and a great opportunity to nurture human intelligence.

From Thebes to Colonus

So, let's go back to Sophocles to decipher the core teaching in his literary bequest: *Oedipus at Colonus.* I repeat, by having Oedipus regain the grace of the gods in Colonus, Sophocles deals with those questions (eluded by modernity) about what to do with the descendants of transgressional families. Indeed, Oedipus' return to grace is synonymous with the absolution of his own transgressions as well as those of his ancestors. For Sophocles, the only possible response is a therapeutic one: we need to heal the heirs of family curses, especially when, like Pericles, they occupy the most important official functions of the city. With *Oedipus at Colonus,* Sophocles offers its citizens a model to allow them to integrate part of their history, that of Pericles, as well as that of the plague epidemic. This is a very important message when considering that they would otherwise be condemned to relive similar disasters[4]. For the final time, Sophocles is assuming the role of guiding the collective conscience that fell to poets and authors of tragic works and was so emblematic of the great Athenian era.

In the healing perspective that belongs to the traditional culture, there is no doubt that Sophocles is referring to the epidemics which devastated Athens when describing the ravages of the plague at the beginning of *Oedipus Rex.* From this angle, he raises and replies to questions about the relationship between the transgenerational legacy of Pericles and the plague which devastated Athens, a disaster he associates with the curse borne by the Labdacids family's last representative, Oedipus.

---

4 Even today, history is still repeating itself with pandemics, the climate threat, pollution and its leaders caught in appearances.

The happy ending of the second play, *Oedipus at Colonus*, contrasts with the desolate scene at the beginning of *Oedipus Rex*. At Colonus, Sophocles completes a journey that refers to successful initiatory trials, the purification of the soul that belongs to many spiritual traditions. In the course of this journey, from Thebes to Colonus, Sophocles reveals his theory of transgenerational principles. He thus leaves us with a formidable therapeutic model on how Oedipus manages to integrate his transgenerational legacies until he is once more deserving of the good graces of the gods. We will study this model by following the stages that characterize Oedipus' healing process.

From this perspective, we can appreciate that with his masterpieces on Oedipus, Sophocles provides the healing model to be applied to the unfinished stories of Pericles and Athens. Although he could not, at the time, save Pericles and Athens, and it took him twenty years to produce this ultimate play; the problem remained an open wound and it was imperative for him to remedy this before bowing out. As with mythology, the poet is inspired by another reality, independent of any chronology. He abandons himself to invisible paths, to this knowledge which operates in him since he had made the paths his own, but which he could hardly have explained in advance and which only appear in the aftermath of the creation.

A Transgenerational Analysis

The transgenerational analysis of the myth that I will present in the following pages will finally provide access behind the scene of Sophocles' plays and entrance to the generally inaccessible backstage area. There, we will discover the presence of a transgenerational structure that underlies both works. The ensuing reinterpretation of the myth radically changes all prior interpretations. It prompts us to reconsider the entire history of Oedipus in a new light.

This revelation of the invisible parts of the myth shows us how Sophocles shared with the ancients a true science of the transgenerational. He recounts the possible consequences of certain transgenerational alienations as well as the benefits of integration work, synonymous with healing and prosperity. This perspective explains the tragic events in *Oedipus Rex* every bit as much as the glorious end of the hero in *Oedipus at Colonus*.

The analysis of this transgenerational dimension in the work of Sophocles will be presented in several stages. In the next chapter, I will introduce the reader to the overall perspective that emerges when one associates both of Sophocles' plays, from Thebes to Colonus.

In the second chapter, I will return to the consciousness of the transgenerational at the time of Sophocles. Whilst the legacy of a family curse was accepted, the issue of acquitting it was not resolved. It is precisely this point that Sophocles illustrates with Oedipus, who ends up integrating his ancestors' debts, thus allowing him to reintegrate the community. With this model, Sophocles explains the nature and stages of the work of integrating transgenerational legacies.

In the third and fourth chapters, we will turn to the origins and history of Thebes. We will recall the events that marked the city, and which were never integrated by its inhabitants. As they did not enter history, these hidden legacies accumulated through the generations, producing ever more dramatic symptomatic effects. Analysis of the debt which alienates Laius and Jocasta will allow us to understand the amplification of the symptoms in this family line towards patricide, incest, and even the tragic destinies of Antigone, Eteocles and Polynices.

In the fifth and sixth chapters we will see how, besides being alienated from his family legacy, Oedipus has also taken on the transgenerational deficiencies of all the Thebans. Those who had chosen him as their king finally condemned him to exile. Such is the destiny of the "king-pharmakos" who is considered a savior one day and a scapegoat the next, responsible for all the misfortune which falls upon the kingdom.

In the seventh chapter, we will see how Oedipus manages to transform his destiny. With the help of Theseus, he will succeed in integrating his transgenerational legacy. Finally, the hero he will become shares with Theseus a secret that will guarantee the prosperity of the latter's kingdom. This apotheosis in Colonus completes the process of transforming plague into prosperity.

In conclusion, I will discuss some of the inherent corollaries of this new interpretation of the myth. It challenges the way we relate to the origins (and Mother Earth) that characterizes our modern civilization. Instead of a conflicting (and alienating) relationship, the perspective of an integration of the world from which we come could preserve harmony with the unwritten laws of the living, a guarantee of prosperity.

I.

From Thebes to Colonus

With such fascinating issues, the history of Oedipus has never failed to inspire creative minds. Thanks to the contributions of countless artists, authors, and philosophers, the myth has been with us since the 5th century B.C. Sigmund Freud turned to it in 1897, when he recognized the value of a legend which, above and beyond the taboos attached to parricide and incest, deals with the limitations of rational thought and heightens the unconscious dimensions of human condition.

An Open Window on the Unconscious

To begin, it is worth recalling the relationships that exist between myths in general, the myth of Oedipus in particular, and the unconscious strata of the psyche, as Freud himself did. A classic example can be found in the relationship between the myth of Oedipus and love stories: a woman complains about discovering that the man she has recently fallen in love with has a problem with alcoholism. Having already suffered through several relationships with alcoholics, she does not understand why this fate seems determined to pursue her. But then she explains that her father was an alcoholic. The relationships of men with their mothers are just as present in those who repeatedly fall in love with a certain kind of person who, upon close inspection, exhibits common characteristics with their mother, and/or similar unfinished and unintegrated stories. For example, people who inherit unresolved grief from their parents may repeatedly develop relationships with individuals who are also unable to grieve and, as a consequence, relive the same unintegrated scenario which has unconsciously alienated them since their childhood.

As the saying goes, love is blind. The Oedipal experience (because that is what this is) forces us to open our eyes to what the child could not perceive about their parents, who they often idealized. Is it a curse to relive these situations or is it just the opposite, an opportunity to be free of them at last? It all depends on how we approach this phenomenon. In best cases scenario, we can look more objectively at the parents and discover who they really are, as when Oedipus discovers the presence of Laius and Jocasta behind Polybius and Merope, the superficial parental imagoes.

Even if tragic, uncovering the truth behind appearances brings with it an expansion of consciousness that can make the difference. This invites new meanings, allowing an individual to process past relationships or events that had not been integrated — the unconscious complexes. Otherwise, if these complexes remain in the shadows, untouched by time, the unintegrated relationship with the parents will continues to weigh on the shoulders of the adult. Children who were too attached to their mother, or too alienated from them, may then have to assume the role of their father instead of living their own life.

By becoming the king of Thebes, Oedipus unconsciously takes upon himself the unfinished stories of his ancestors and finds himself in the bed of his mother Jocasta. The myth illustrates how his alienation drives Oedipus to find himself in the position of his father, that is to say, to be someone other than himself. In this sense, and as we will analyze below, for the community, Oedipus becomes the unconscious representative of his father, Laius, who died in unclear circumstances and whose grief has not been mourned. Incest and parricide are symbolical and theatrical ways to illustrate the alienation of Oedipus from his true Self. From a mythological point of view, Oedipus is parricidal and incestuous until he rebirths as a true Self, and until that happens he remains trapped in his matrix of omnipotence. From Thebes to Colonus, Sophocles invites us to follow the history of the metamorphosis of Oedipus through his second birth, this time as his true Self[1].

Why are modern thinkers unable to identify this metamorphosis as the central message of Sophocles, even though it is perfectly in tune with the times? Are they blinded by their own oedipal complex, or by the way our modern culture has conditioned us all? Indeed, in our culture, the most common "resolution" of the Oedipal complex consists of repressing one's Oedipus apparent drives in order to align with the so-called reality principle. This is disenchanting, to say the least. Freud showed in what way and under what circumstances a

---

[1] The original French text employs the word "sujet", literally "subject", to refer to this particular aspect of one's being, following French usage in the field of philosophy and psychoanalysis. However, in English, the word "subject" appears sometimes to have a meaning which is quite different. Thus, we have adopted the word "Self" for "sujet", sometimes modified as "true Self" or "deep Self" or "inner Self". This "Self" is different from any other forms of being that would result from external influences. It is the very core of ourselves, which cannot be divided, possessing the inalterable quality of wholeness and of inalienability because of its privileged relation to the present moment over any past incidents.

new entity, the *superego*, evolves in the mind that has successfully repressed its Oedipal apparent pulsion and abandoned the potential development of the true Self. "Normal" neurosis then sets in, leaving the person in a state of unconscious conflict, convinced that reality should be a certain way (as most people are) and condemned to keep sublimating or repressing their unconscious Oedipal conflicts. Thus, the conditions are satisfied for the transmission of this problem to future generations who, in turn, will try to repress it following the example of their parents. In this way, the "Oedipus complex" develops into a collective norm that characterizes our modern civilization.

Restoring Sophocles' True Purpose

But when we avoid projecting our own modern biases, we are forced to recognize that Sophocles presents us with a completely different option. Too formatted by the collective model of the repression of the Oedipus complex, Sophocles' perspective escapes modern minds. In truth, Sophocles' masterpieces have nothing in common with the way we have understood Oedipal issues so far. His purpose is about individual and collective healing, and he uses the art of tragedy to illustrate how to handle the worst of our fate as mere mortals, proposing an exercise in alchemy that can only work for those who live by the unwritten laws that govern the world, particularly those that regulate transgenerational inheritance.

The option taken by Sophocles is conform to the ancient "religious" and initiatory traditions, which today correspond to certain forms of personal or spiritual development practiced by a minority. As we will discover with the transgenerational analysis of the myth of Oedipus that will follow, Sophocles is rooted in a therapeutic tradition that was well aware of the consequences of family curses. To heal is not a question of repressing the problem as moderns people have learned to do, but rather of crossing it, from Thebes to Colonus, to reframe and integrate one's transgenerational inheritance and reveal the true Self. This opens a path that leads to learning about our true Self and which allows Oedipus to answer the famous question: who am I?

Although it doesn't seem this way, the real desire of Oedipus is to emerge as a true Self, to answer the inner call for self-knowledge. This is a desire that is incomparably more essential than what modern people reduce to the will to simply replace his father in his mother's bed. To access this more complete perspective, we need to contemplate both of Sophocles' plays on Oedipus. We should also be wary of how our modern minds are fascinated with breaking taboos and how that could make us reduce the symbolic dimension of the art, as if it were a true story. It would then become more difficult to take this lucid look at the theme, to which we aspire.

With *Oedipus at Colonus*, Sophocles shows that the real goal of Oedipus has nothing to do with satisfying supposed desires of incest and parricide, even if unconscious. To reduce Oedipus this would be tantamount to Laius and Jocasta relieving their unconscious transference needs onto the back of the child. To interpret Oedipal fantasies as authentic desires lets the tragedy invade our daily lives – as modern civilization does. On the other hand, if we stick to the story itself, we understand that, for Oedipus, the transgression of taboos was the only way for him to discover the secret about his adoption, a secret which unconsciously alienated him. Those whom he mistook for his parents, Polybius and Merope, had kept his adoption secret. This point matters more than any other because it prevented Oedipus from integrating the story of his origins, that of his real family. On the other hand, once he discovered it, fortified by a non-alienated awareness of his origins (and therefore of himself), he could finally come to term with his prehistory and emerge as a true Self.

In this regard, the transgression of taboos is secondary when compared to Oedipus' alienation and his need to free himself and all the Thebans from the consequences of the secret of his birth. Because it is symbolic, mythology offers a way to face our worst fear, and, as tragic as they may be, parricide and incest are really just secondary to the core issue. In the aftermath, these transgressions appear from another angle, that of an exit from that incestuous and parricide position that prevailed until now because Oedipus had not yet been born as a subject.

With Oedipus discovering its true origins and which will reborn in Colonus, Sophocles perfectly illustrates the famous injunction of another famous Greek poet, Pindar: "Become such as you are, having learned what that is! "

From this overall perspective, including the second play *Oedipus in Colonus*, it appears that oedipal impulses are not the result of a genuine desire. Rather, Oedipus' behavior (love for the mother and rivalry with the father) embodies the tribulations of an alienated person who is prisoner of his transgenerational inheritance that prevents him from becoming truly himself. In other words, these are the symptoms of a being not yet born as a subject – something that is common in our modern culture. The mythological staging of incest and parricide allows us to recognize the immaturity of Oedipus in order to cure him, rather than dramatize his fantasies and behaviors.

At the end of the journey, in Colonus, Sophocles associates the metamorphosis of Oedipus with the return to grace with the gods, to testify he had finished paying for the transgenerational debts he inherited at birth.

Reaching the End of the Process

At the end of his journey, Oedipus becomes an accomplished Self, freed from transgenerational alienations. Having reconnected with fertile origins, he now enters history and collective memory. In this context we are better able to understand the meaning of his last recommendation of remembrance, a resonance with ancient tradition: "Do not forget me, even dead, if you want prosperity to remain your lot forever. "

Curiously, this glorious finale is little known to the public at large. All too often Sophocles' second play, *Oedipus at Colonus*, is put aside as if everything began and ended at Thebes and as if it would be impossible for Oedipus to overcome his tragedy and live out any future at all. And yet the apotheosis of *Oedipus at Colonus* clarifies the Oedipal destiny and is especially useful for understanding the Oedipus myth. This illustrates a classic process to which mythological heroes have been subjected. Joseph Campbell[2], for example, deciphered a common structure, the monomyth, which illustrates the rite of passage into the adult world: it symbolizes the necessary maturation of the Self, the death of its old "ego", and its moving forward with a new identity. To ignore Sophocles' second play devoted to Oedipus would deprive us of an essential part of his message.

---

[2] Joseph Campbell, *The Hero with a Thousand Faces*, 2008, New World Library, Novato, California.

In his analysis of *Oedipus Rex*, André Bonnard leaves the door open to Colonus. He is sufficiently perspicacious not to give in to the facile interpretation of typically modern morality, which would be at odds with the symbolic nature of the myth (maintaining that tragedy results from the principal character's flawed behavior). His commentary on the final scene of *Oedipus Rex* presages the new destiny that Sophocles will propose in *Oedipus at Colonus*: "But look at this creature who staggers and gropes his way forward. Is he truly annihilated? [...] No. No Greek tragedy - not even Oedipus - ever invited the Athenian public to such resignation, to raise the white flag of surrender. Beyond the apparent cries of despair, the protestations of abandonment, we will find this "spiritual strength" which is at the core of the unbreakable resistance of this old man (Sophocles-Oedipus) and his people. We can already feel that life fights on in this creature who had been consigned to annihilation and takes up its march again. Oedipus is going to gather up these stones which Destiny has heaped upon him and use them as new weapons: he lives on to fight again, but with a more accurate perspective on his human condition. [...] Slowly we become aware that the plot, however terribly it weighed upon us, was not leading us to the hero's utter ruin, but was instead making us wait, and reach deep within ourselves, throughout the entire play, for something unknown, both feared and hoped for, for this response from Oedipus to these gods that had beaten him down."[3]

---

3 André Bonnard, *Civilisation grecque*, tome II, 1954, La Guilde du Livre, Lausanne, p. 97-98.

Renewal

The response which Sophocles sends to the gods goes like this: by integrating his origins and letting his old life die, Oedipus atones for his flaws and those of his ancestors. This kind of emancipation and rebirth correspond to spiritual journeys which are found in the ancient sacred texts. For example, in the *Corpus Hermeticum*[4] we find: "Seek out the guide who will show you the path which leads to the doors of understanding, there where the light shines the brightest, freed of all obscurity [...] But first, you must tear in pieces the tunic that you are wearing, the cloth of ignorance, the tool of malice, the chain of corruption, the shadowy jail, the living death, the living corpse, the tomb which you carry with you everywhere, the thief who abides in the house, the companion who, by what he loves, hates you, and by what he hates, envies you." Such a description of this other in one's Self whose presence suffocates its deepest being corresponds to the manifold forms of alienation that Oedipus must emancipate himself from to become truly himself.

At Colonus, the gods will grant their graces to the former king of Thebes, now cured of his alienation. Oedipus can then offer his guests this invaluable guarantee of prosperity. The rebirth which Sophocles invites us to witness corresponds to the emergence of the Self in Oedipus, a being who offers to man his full dimension, embodied as this new hero, as a benefactor to his hosts. Georges Méautis also emphasizes the importance of the transformation of Oedipus: "The *Ajax* and the *Oedipus Rex* show the suffering and agony of the hero, as his human nature is annihilated so that his more-than-human

---

4 Hermès Trismégiste, Corpus Hermeticum, tome 1, 2011, Les Belles Lettres, Paris, p. 81-82.

nature could germinate, [...] *Oedipus at Colonus*, shows the victory of this divine force, the hero, over these creatures that surround him. A beggar, miserable because he has lived through the "dark night", been rejected, humiliated, and looked upon as an object of horror, becomes the prize of a battle between states, the fruits of happiness and prosperity for these he favors."[5] Such a rebirth also corresponds to the ancestral purpose of initiation, religious elevation which explains Oedipus' return to grace.

Regarding this glorious ending, we should need to recall the events at the beginning of the first play, *Oedipus Rex*, to discover the central and overarching theme of the myth. Sophocles' story begins with the description of a plague that causes animals, people, and even crops to become sterile. And, as we noted above, after his exile, from Thebes to Colonus, Oedipus bequeaths to his hosts a secret that will guarantee their prosperity. The plague and the infertility of Laius and Jocasta, and Merope and Polybius, can be added to the picture painted by Sophocles to find the unifying transgenerational theme of the myth, of movement from infertility to fertility[6].

The thems of fertility was very common in the vast and complex mythological culture of classical Greece, nourished by stories and legends in neighboring countries. In matriarchal societies, for example, where the function of the father was hidden and ignored, we can find the Oedipal theme when

---

[5] Georges Méautis, *Sophocle, essai sur le héros tragique*, 1957, Albin Michel, Paris, p. 171.

[6] The issue of fertility clearly concerns symbolic productivity. Fertile thinking guaranties the integration of one's own experience, a fundamental activity of the true self, being the expression of life, the permanent renewal of self-knowledge, a never-ending process.

a boy was called to replace his father and fertilize Mother Earth (Demeter) to guarantee the renewal of life.

Mircea Eliade[7] reminds us that in all the great myths of the East, entry into immortal life was guaranteed to those who succeeded in overcoming the trials of descent into the depths of Mother Earth - to the source of life. This return to Mother Earth, in the person of Jocasta for Oedipus, resembles the rites of passage of children (in caves) who sacrificed their childhood to begin adult life. Near Athens, but originally from Egypt, the Eleusinian Mysteries depicted the passage from life to death and vice versa. For Joseph Campbell, the cult of Demeter at Eleusis was associated with the "cycles of death" and, "the descent into hell and the resurrection. This idea was symbolized by the agrarian cycle; death by harvesting, followed by sowing the seed and the growth of plants. In other words, the spiritual message is conveyed by using agrarian imagery"[8].

This theme is also central to Sophocles' work. His very first play dealt with the young Triptolemus, prince of Eleusis, who was initiated by his mother Demeter into the mysteries of the cycles of life and renewal. With Oedipus guaranteeing prosperity in his birth town of Colonus, Sophocles could not have completed his life and his work better, leaving behind a (secret) teaching synonymous with prosperity for those who deserve it, as Oedipus did for Theseus.

Numerous associations can also be made between the Egyptian Sphinx, the Ethiopian Phoenix, and the Sphinx in the Oedipus myth. Always rising from its ashes, the Phoenix

---

7 Mircea Eliade, *Rites and Symbols of Initiation (Birth and Rebirth)*, Harvill Press, 1958, London.

8 Joseph Campbell, *Transformation of Myth Through Time*, 1999, Harper Perennia, New York.

is a symbol par excellence of the rebirth process and can be associated with Oedipus who dies as a king to be reborn as the future hero of Colonus.

Reconnecting to the Origins

The radical metamorphosis of Oedipus corresponds to spiritual transformation. The prophecy the seer Tiresias told Oedipus, "This day will see your birth and death all at once", referring to the process of the development of the Self as an initiation into self-knowledge. Tiresias' revelation may seem paradoxical at first glance, but it corresponds to the transformation that can take place in transgenerational therapy.

At the beginning of *Oedipus Rex*, not knowing who he really is, Oedipus is quite simply not himself. Everything he tried to do until that point was not done by an authentic Oedipus. He was too alienated to be aware, a victim of divine destiny, contrary to what he could have believed. Oedipus was functioning in sacrificial mode, which I venture to call the *nirvana style*[9]. Unable to integrate his unconscious transgenerational legacy, he turns it back upon its origins - a behavior that attests to the absence of a Self, and which ultimately produces the drama, all around him, from what resides in the depths of his true Self: the plague. The latter can thus be understood as an echo of the parental infertility he inherited at birth. Oedipus is encircled by the plague in the same way he was by infertile parents - to the extent that they were incapable of giving birth to his true Self - and who did not take long to decide to get rid of him. Sophocles begins his

[9] The *nirvana style* refers to behaviors that do not manifest the individual will of a person, but are the result of a transgenerational legacy which plays itself out in spite of him, thus alienating him. A proposed definition of the *nirvana style* is found in the Glossary.

story on the very day that Oedipus will discover this truth, the day his origins will be revealed to him, the day the veil which alienated his inner Self will fall away. This discovery will transform a life characterized by the *nirvana style* into another existence, more authentic and more individualized. The tragedy told at the end of *Oedipus Rex* will then take on the birth of the Self in Oedipus, a necessary step on the way to the final emancipation of the hero by the end of *Oedipus at Colonus*.

Sophocles' perspective has nothing in common with the modern approach to Oedipus which condemns his relationship with his mother on the basis that it is incestuous[10]. Thus, modern culture biases and dramatizes the Oedipal initiation, obstructing the pathway towards the emergence of the Self. Sophocles explains in his last play how Oedipus reconnects with the collective at a more essential level, a more human level, where everyone can recognize each other as true selves as Theseus does when he recognizes Oedipus' true Self and decides to accommodate him. This return to himself, as his true Self, corresponds to the harmonious restoration of his relation with the world and with others, according to the famous motto of the ancient Greeks: "Know thyself and you will know the gods and the universe."

Oedipus' transformation from an alienated life to becoming the benefactor of Colonus corresponds at every step to the stages of integration of transgenerational legacies. This process, therefore, does not involve an egocentric operation that would lead the person to cut himself off from others and his origins. The contrast between Oedipus' two lives also provides insight into Sophocles' definition of adulthood. As

---

[10] Of course, Sophocles plays with those biases to produce the desired and optimal emotional outcome.

much as he was a king in Thebes, Oedipus did not know himself. In the eyes of an ancient sage, Oedipus the king was not yet a man.

To Respect the Symbolism of the Myth

This symbolic approach to transgenerational integration therapy is necessary to understand the links to origins without excluding fusion with the mother and absence of the father. In the language of myth, incest and parricide are tools allowing us to grasp an invisible reality and clarify the nature of what is transmitted from one generation to another. Faced with these two taboos, a non-symbolic approach would encounter considerable difficulties. In other words, it is a matter of relativizing rational discourse, or "logos", to penetrate the symbolic nature of mythology, its own discourse, or even its "mythos".

The reader will understand that, in psychological parlance, the terms *incest* and *parricide* are not reference to a truly incestuous relationship, and even less so to the crime of murder. Rather, they evoke a profound symbolic and generally invisible reality that is related to the absence or presence of a true Self. Such language allows us to grapple with certain truths related to the life of the soul, and to interpret situations whose meaning goes beyond reason alone. Depth psychology and transgenerational therapy share this symbolic language with mythology as a way of coping with unwritten laws and understanding their role in our destiny. All things considered, the evolution that we observe from the alienated life of Oedipus to his beneficial role at Colonus corresponds to the transgenerational integration process that we observe in therapy.

In symbolic language or *Mythos*, chaotic love, irrational situations, and symptoms do not repeat themselves: they are and remain present, sometimes in the shadows, sometimes in the light of day. But whether these experiences are hidden away or denied, they are an integral part of life. They remain present until the day they enter personal or collective history and become available to memory as a source of teaching rather than as a subject to be avoided. Meanwhile, un-integrated experiences are the source of questions that leads us to greater self-knowledge and growth as true Selves. This is what the Oedipus myth evokes: an unconscious relationship to one's origins (parents, ancestors and archetypes) which demands to be integrated and humanized.

In this perspective, the Oedipus myth illustrates the unconscious determinism of transgenerational inheritance before unveiling the potential for the true Self to transform the situation.

The Universal Matrix

In the myth, incest does not, therefore, refer so much to a supposed sexual relationship as to the recognition of an original symbiosis from which Oedipus would not yet have emerged, however much of a king he may have been. Marie Delcourt[11] also explains that the theme of union with the mother is reduced by modern interpretation, as with the Freudian interpretation, when really it carries a much deeper traditional meaning: union with Mother-Earth. Mircea Eliade also reminds us that certain American myths reveal

[11] Marie Delcourt (1981), *Œdipe ou la légende du conquérant*, Les Belles Lettres, Paris.

origin stories: "in illo tempore: the first men lived for a certain time in the womb of their Mother, that is to say in the bowel of the Earth. There, in the telluric depths, they led a half-human life as embryos still imperfectly formed. [...] According to these myths, although the Creator had already prepared all the things for them on the surface of the Earth, he nevertheless decided that humans would remain hidden for some time in the belly of their telluric Mother, to develop better, to mature."[12] Symbolically, the first part of Oedipus' life corresponds to an immature being which calls for a second birth, that of the true Self which happens in Colonus.

Perhaps it should also be remembered that in shamanic culture there are three distinct worlds: the underworld, the middle world, and the upper world. The incestuous child would be a prisoner of the underworld, still in the womb, waiting to be step into broad daylight and settle between earth and sky.

In Thebes, these three worlds are deeply un-balanced. Cadmus had fathered two descendant lines unable to live together. By planting the teeth of a dragon in the ground he gave birth to his first offspring, the Spartoi or the Sowed Ones. Born of the earth, they were akin to the underworld. His second lineage was linked to the upper world because he fathered it with the goddess Harmonia. These two family branches never cease to confront each other in their attempts to seize the throne and the situation causes a plague which threatens to annihilate everything. At the end of his life, Oedipus succeeds in rebalancing these worlds by reconnecting with the fertile, non-dual unity that guarantees prosperity.

---

[12] Mircea Eliade (1987), *The Sacred and The Profane*, Harcourt Brace Jovanovich.

II

A Transgenerational Curse

In antiquity, everybody knew that faults committed by one or more parents devolve upon their descendants. The awareness of such transgenerational unwritten laws can be perceived in the very ancient tradition of ancestor worship. Since the first, primal, shamanic societies and in all traditional cultures, peoples have honored the memory of these intergenerational links for reasons that can only be misunderstood by modern minds.

Ancient Awareness of Transgenerational Heritages

Ancients texts testify to this awareness of what can be transmitted through the generations. The Bible is littered with such references, for example, Jeremiah (31, 29), "The fathers eat sour grapes, and the children's teeth are set on edge".

An extract from *The Iliad*[1] illustrates the respect for intergenerational ties among the ancient Greeks. On the battlefield during the Trojan War, the Trojan Glaucus encountered a Greek enemy Diomedes. But they discover that Diomedes grandfather, Oneus, once offered hospitality to Glaucus' grandfather, Bellerophon. Thus, linked by the good relations

[1] Homer, *The Iliad*, chant VI.

of their respective grandfathers, Glaucus and Diomedes decide to honor the ancestral friendship and, instead of confronting each other, to exchange their armor as a sign of mutual respect.

Gustave Glotz was fascinated by those transgenerational heritages he characterized as "natural solidarity." It connected children to the history of their parents as new branches of a tree are connected to the trunk and roots. “One cannot fail to remark family resemblances in terms of traits and character. We observe the transmission of illnesses, of madness, of warts and birthmarks. How could one fail to observe the inheritance of moral faults? The son cannot detach himself from his father, as any work from its creator: he carries within himself a part of his author. Evildoers pass on to their children the essential elements of their personality, and these elements do not remain passive: those who have received them live off of them, nourish themselves with them, and find in them the substance of their thoughts as well as the motives for their actions.... Sometimes divine punishment indeed spares not only the guilty but even his immediate descendants, only to fall upon his great-nephews; these are the thunderclaps striking from afar which so overwhelmed the honest Herodotus.”[2]

As is so often mentioned concerning Oedipus, the Greeks invoked an *ate,* a curse or malediction which pursued the members of a family across several generations for the faults of their forbears. Jacqueline de Romilly stresses this transgenerational principle in the works of another famous

---

[2] Gustave Glotz (1904), *La solidarité dans la famille Grecque*, Albert Fontemoing, Paris, p. 580.

tragedian, Euripides: "The fact is that the subject of the tragedy of the *Bacchaes* is the punishment which God inflicts for a fault which was committed by the preceding generation."[3]

The ancient Greeks thought that if a man was not punished for a fault which he committed during his life, his descendants would suffer the consequences. In this regard, Eric Dodds explains that "Theogones complained that a system was unjust if it "allowed a criminal to escape while someone else suffers his punishment later on" [....] This could appear unjust, but it seemed to them to be a law of nature which one must accept: the family was a moral unit, the life of the son being a prolongation of the life of the father, such that he inherited the moral deficits of his father just as he inherited his commercial debts. Sooner or later the debt insisted on being paid: as the *Pythian* foretold to Croesus, the causal connection between the crime and the punishment was *moira*, something which even a god could not break with; Croesus would have to bring to an end or fulfill what had been provoked by the crime of an ancestor who lived five generations before him."[4]

The same transgenerational principles apply to Oedipus. As we analyze in detail in the following chapters, he had inherited the non-integrated events and the faults of his ancestors that impacted the first part of his life. The transgenerational heritages that alienated Oedipus were passed down through several generations. The problematic heritage of Oedipus started with the first succession to the throne of Cad-

---

3 Jacqueline de Romilly (1971), *Le temps dans la tragédie Grecque*, Vrin, Paris, pp. 101-102.
4 Eric Dodds *(1959), The Greeks and the Irrational,* University of California Press, Berkeley.

mus, his illustrious ancestor. Indeed, this family will be traumatized by dramas never integrated, unresolved griefs, wrongful actions, the infanticide of Pentheus in particular, whose consequences accumulate over the generations and finally are transmitted to Oedipus through Laius and Jocasta.

The tragedy of Oedipus concentrates all the problems that were repressed and denied by his ancestors. These events, mired in suffering and non-integrated conflicts, are amplified from one generation to the next, creating an accumulation that will sooner or later demands redress of the transgenerational debt. This accumulation leads to that infamous day designated by Tiresias as the day on which Oedipus will die and be born at one and the same time, a pivotal day enabling us to distinguish the first part of Oedipus' life (playing out the drama of all the problems which he inherited) from the second part of his destiny which will see him integrate this heritage to transform it into a source of benefits for his last hosts.

The misinterpretation of the Oracle

The legacies which Laius and Jocasta pass down to their child were announced by the oracle even before Oedipus was born. Apparently, no one could interpret its words. When Laius asked the gods, the oracle announced that, if he persisted in wanting to have a son, his son would kill him, commit incest, and be the cause of great misery. But what is the real message from the gods behind this disturbing message?

If the message of the oracle conveys this absolute truth, what the ancient Greeks called *Alètheia*, it is still necessary not to misunderstand it. The truth here concerns the man's true Self, its authentic, even divine part, which neither Laius nor Jocasta can figure out. Only the seers or initiate can access this order of knowledge which includes simultaneously what was, what is and what will be.

Behind the prophecy of the consequences for Laius, if he persists in wanting to have a son, there is a hidden message about the real cause of his infertility. This message is yet to be understood and is certainly not independent of the tragedies which are predicted. On hearing it better, the oracle indicates the deep nature of Laius and Jocasta's problem: since their son cannot be born as a true Self, he can only be incestuous and parricidal to the extent that, deprived of the parental "verb" which would allow it, he will be unable to leave the matrix (incest) and thus will be excluded from any relationship with the father.

The Prisoner of a Symbolic Matrix

To be heard, the message of the oracle calls for a particular, hermeneutic and symbolic attention. This allows us to grasp several levels of reality, starting from what is apparent (superficial or conscious) to other meanings, generally hidden and inaccessible to those who do not speak the symbolic language. Beyond what it says, the oracle announces the state of the true Self in Oedipus, symbolically stillborn. Imprisoned in a closed matrix, the Self within Oedipus remains the tributary of a symbiotic - or incestuous - relationship where the father is absent, or like a dead man, the very image of what is wrong with Jocasta and Laius. Their parental function is brought into question to the extent that, being themselves excessively alienated by their ancestors, they are unable to pass down anything other than their own unconscious conflicts and heritages.

Peter Szondi explains that "the oracle does not present itself as a warning [...] Without having been forbidden, beforehand, to father a son, Laius must learn that he will be killed by his son. This knowledge, unlike the warning, leaves no room for salvation. No action can correspond to it; if it incites the killing of the son, it also reveals the vanity of such an act: in it, salvation and unreason are one. Whether Laius believes in the oracle or not (Jocasta will later opt for disbelief) does not change the situation."[5]

Facing the oracle's words, it is not a question of deciding on any action. As in-depth psychology, the only way to proceed would be to penetrate the meaning of the words of the oracle, to fully hear it. For a transgenerational analyst, the answer is simple: if Oedipus is incestuous and parricidal before even being born, it is the fact of parents too alienated to give birth to the Self of the child. If they had wanted to understand the message of the oracle, rather than having a child, Laius and Jocasta would have been concerned first of all to become true selves themselves, to integrate their own transgenerational alienation. Instead of doing this work on themselves, they simply transfer their own shortcomings to the future child.

Sophocles warns us here. If even kings and queens are no longer capable of introspection to understand the oracle, what can we expect from this new civilization which is just now beginning to develop?

The words of the oracle are polysemous, to have a chance to understand its true meanings one must speak its symbolic language as if it were a dream truly experienced.

---

5 Peter Szondi, (2002), *An Essay on the Tragic*, Stanford University Press.

For those, like Laius and Jocasta, who do not have access to their unconscious world, it is difficult to grasp the meaning of the words of the oracle. By reducing his message, taken literally, they even run the risk of making it a self-fulfilling prophecy. And because Laius and Jocasta only find there one occasion to project on Oedipus their own unconscious conflicts, the oracular word will turn against them. Instrumentalized to relieve their own unconscious transference needs, they have diverted the oracle from its depths and perverted its meaning. Far from integrating the origin of their sterility issue, they continue to ignore their difficulties by projecting them onto Oedipus. Thus, and paradoxically, the oracle causes the birth of Oedipus. The transgenerational debt responsible for the sterility of Laius and Jocasta is neither understood nor integrated, but simply shifted to the future child, even before birth, henceforth destined to be parricidal and incestuous.

Interestingly enough, Oedipus will repeat this scenario which consists of taking upon himself the sterility of his surroundings when, as king of Thebes, he decides to solve the problem of the plague at all costs. In other words, when he takes responsibility for the problem of the plague (including the infertility it produces), he then renews the experience of being born of an infertile context, but this time to be reborn.

The false resolution of parental sterility will have new, even more, dramatic consequences. Indeed, it will come back to the fore when the plague falls on Thebes. Oedipus then relives the scenario of its origins and appropriates it by deciding, whatever the cost, to solve the problem. He once again takes upon himself he shortcomings of his entourage, parents and all Thebans combined. In other words, he repeats his experience of being born of a sterile couple.

III

The Heritage of Laius

After having recalled the context of the time and after having associated the two plays that Sophocles devotes to Oedipus to unveil the overall perspective from Thebes to Colonus, it is now time to get to the heart of the matter, that is to say, to the analysis of Oedipus' transgenerational heritages. This starts by going up the paternal branch, that of Laius and Labdacids, all the way to Cadmus, the founder of Thebes. Once the heritages from his father's side is clarified, we will turn, in the following chapter, to the side of maternal filiation to analyze the inheritances transmitted by Jocasta, and also return to Cadmus, the common ancestor.

Developing Freudian interpretations, new studies have added the history of Laius, his problematic of being a "bad" father and his role in the destiny of his son. Indeed, before Oedipus kills this father whom he did not know, it should be recalled that in the first place it was Laius who tried to eliminate his son, three days after his birth. This infanticidal attempt is an important element that helps us recapture what went wrong in the paternal lineage. This part of the history opens a new door and allows us to better understand the transmission of the curse along this family line. To take into consideration Laius' role is a first step of the transgenerational analysis of the Oedipus legacies that have accumulated over generations since Cadmus, the founder of Thebes.

The Unfinished Story of Laius

One of the most important aspects of understanding the burden which Laius places on his child relates to an inglorious episode in his history. It concerns his responsibility for the suicide of Chrysippus, the son of his host and protector, King Pelops. Laius had taken refuge in the house of King Pelops after a rival line had seized power in Thebes upon the death of his father, King Labdacus. "There, he developed a passionate attachment to Chrysippus, the young son of Pelops, and, according to some sources, thereupon invented unnatural forms of love"[1]. He carried off and abused the adolescent, who then killed himself for shame. After these events, Pelops prayed to the gods that justice be done.

In 1953, George Devereux had already analyzed the relationship between Laius' abuse of Chrysippus and Laius' desire to get rid of Oedipus. He explained that, according to some versions of the myth, "the oracle at Delphi tells Laius that Zeus has decided that his son would kill him as the punishment for the rape of Chrysippus. This curse suggests that, in the Greek understanding, the figure of Oedipus is linked to that of Chrysippus - an association which is also implicit in another version of the myth wherein Hera, enraged by the dramatic events involving Chrysippus, sends the Sphinx to

---

[1] Pierre Grimal, *Dictionnaire de la mythologie grecque et romaine*, 1969, PUF, Paris.

punish the Thebans for having tolerated Laius' abusive behavior."[2]

As we can see, the former events and the curse called down by Pelops explain a part of what returns unconsciously in the mind of Laius when he confronts Oedipus. As we observed in the previous chapter, Laius does not understand the oracle which would require of him the integration of his own unfinished stories before even thinking having a child. Taken literally, the word of the oracle traps him and reinforces his shortcomings. Believing that Oedipus would want to kill him justifies bequeathing generationally his own curse.

The intentions that the father attributes to his son, even before his birth, inform us about what is transmitted between Laius and Oedipus. These intentions invite us to examine how Laius tried to rid himself of the transgenerational inheritance he failed to assume and which he will therefore transmit to his son.

John Munder Ross would say of Laius that his representation of his son is "the distorted product of his paranoia, revealing the frightful projective identification of the father.[...] His egocentricity and his brutality turn a potentially loving and respectful son into a stranger and an enemy, in such a way that the prophecy of parricide becomes self-fulfilling."[3]

---

[2] Georges Devereux, "Why Oedipus killed Laius: a note on the complementary Oedipus complex", in *International Journal of psycho-analysis*, n°34, p. 132-141.
[3] John Munder Ross "Oedipus revisited, Laius and the Laius complex" in *Psychoanalytic Studies of the Child*, vol. 37, 1982, p. 179-180.

Failing to understand the oracle, Laius makes use of it to justify his crime against his descendants. Georges Devereux[4] proposes to define this situation as the "Laius complex".

Marie Balmary also insists on the fact that Laius is not able to become a father when he condemns his son to death. "No one occupies his proper place around Oedipus. His father denied being his father when he wanted to kill Oedipus. His mother, by going along with this plan, hardly stands in a better relationship with him. His adoptive parents, who pretend to be his birth parents, are also inadequate. Ultimately Oedipus' only true relationship is concerning the symptoms of his own body: his swollen feet."[5] By hanging him from his feet, his father effectively leaves behind a clue to his attempted infanticide, one which becomes the origin of his name since Oedipus means: "swollen feet".

However it may be, even if Laius condemns Oedipus to death upon the slopes of Mount Cithaeron, hanging from his feet at the mercy of savage beasts, history tells us that Oedipus will be saved by a shepherd and then adopted by Polybius and Merope, king and queen of Corinth. We note that the problem of affiliation which characterizes the Labdacids is repeated in the adoption of Oedipus: if Polybius and Merope decide to adopt him, it is because they also suffer from infertility. They, too, fail to take responsibility for their difficulties since they harbor a secret that will leave the Self within Oedipus at an impasse. Deprived of the truth, Oedipus will only learn the truth about his origins by returning to Thebes, his birthplace, an obligatory symbolic rite of passage to be reborn as his true Self.

---

[4] Georges Devereux, *Essais d'ethnopsychiatrie générale*, troisième édition, 1977, Gallimard, Paris, p. 168.
[5] Marie Balmary, *L'homme aux statues*, 1979, Grasset, Paris, p. 42.

Laius' abuse of the young Chrysippus also reveals that he was incapable of distinguishing[6] between the sexes and of respecting the sequence of generations since Chrysippus was still a young adolescent. Alain Fine emphasizes the consequences of this lack of distinctions: "Certainly Laius is a pedophile in the myth; he is depicted as acting upon and acted upon by an uncontrolled sexuality, notably homosexual, due to his hubris[7]. His abuse of Chrysippus reveals some potential for incestuous father/son relations on the part of Laius who does not take into account either the differences between the genders nor the differences between generations."[8]

This confusion between generations should be understood as a sign of one aspect of Laius' alienation, the personalized form of his transgenerational legacies. It is not surprising to learn further that the reason for the infertility of Laius and Jocasta couple is also linked to his inability to perform heterosexual activities. Jocasta had to get Laius drunk to perform the sexual act which would bring about the birth of Oedipus.

Apart from the exposure of his pedophilia, Laius' problems also concern the phenomenon of birth. This theme is not unrelated to the need to fulfill one's mourning so that life can reassert its rightful place again. Moreover, the theme of

[6] Not a superficial differentiation, but understood as the product of an operative symbolization, that is to say, functioning like a veritable kind of practical knowledge.

[7] *Hubris*: everything which is immoderate, excessive ardor, getting carried away, abusive behavior, insults, physical abuse, also used in the sense of an offense against the natural order of things.

[8] Alain Fine, "Laïos pédophile et infanticide", in *Revue Française de Psychanalyse*, tome LVII, avril-juin, 1993, PUF, Paris.

sexual differences and birth are intimately related. In this regard, Jacqueline Schaeffer[9] points out: "The difference between the sexes is the first difference, the paradigm for all the other differences. It is through the difference of the sexes that the infant comes into the world. The first questioning glance upon a child asks what its sexual gender is. It is the perception of the difference between the sexes which pushes the child, as we know, into intensive thinking which leads it to come up with infantile theories of sexuality." Unable to integrate that dimension of reality and let it operate, Laius is not able to enjoy heterosexual relations with Jocasta.

Beyond the events related to the death of Chrysippus are there other factors that would explain why Laius could not be an edifying father? Could the absence of an inner Self be the symptom of a deficiency which he inherited from his ancestors?

If the fault of Laius and the curse of Pelops partly explain the curse inherited by Oedipus, it is indeed also necessary to better understand the problematic of Laius, the one from which he, too, inherits from his ancestors. We will, therefore, deepen the question to go beyond the explanations, beyond the stigmatization of a parent, to embrace a broader perspective, properly transgenerational, to include the relationship to origins.

---

[9] Jacqueline Schaeffer, *La différence des sexes dans le couple ou la cocréation du masculin et du féminin*, 2003. Conference cycle on the introduction to adult psychoanalysis, published on the website www.spp.asso.fr

Unaccomplished Griefs in the Labdacids Lineage

There are further unfinished stories among the Labdacids, which deserve analysis, in order to fully expound the transgenerational heritage of Oedipus. The true cause of Laius' infertility comes to the fore when one analyzes the family line of the Labdacids. One phenomenon recurs: the disappearance of the fathers in the childhood of the sons and the inability of the sons to mourn their fathers. In effect, the mourning of the father does not take place among the Labdacids, and this failing is passed down and amplified from one generation to another. Let us analyze in more detail the way the infertility of Laius is an inheritance of unresolved grief.

One of the first kings of Thebes in this family line was Polydorus, son of Cadmus and the goddess, Harmonia. The premature death of Polydorus leaves behind his very young son, Labdacus. Here we find the beginning of the absence of a relationship between fathers and sons, which then becomes recurrent in the line of Labdacids. Cleopatra Athanassiou analyzes this series thus: "When the time comes, Labdacus himself, in turn, will die, leaving behind a very young son, Laius. Where does this leave us, this break between the father and son, such that the son cannot benefit from the presence of a father to guide him from early childhood into adolescence? Why would a father not be there while his son is growing up until the time of sexual maturity? It is not arbitrary to posit the hypothesis that a meeting is impossible at the moment where a one on one conflict becomes a possibility, at this point of a heritage which can be traced back to the loves of Zeus and Io, the moment of the brutal confrontation with an intolerable truth or of a conflict whose violence could destroy both antagonists, not just one or the other, thereby suppressing the very conditions which would bring up the conflict. As it is, the two participants in the conflict survive just a brief moment together, outside the domain of sexuality which would bring them into conflict. And there is one final avoidance: the infant Oedipus will be sent far away, to the top of Mount Cithaeron, before returning to fall upon his father and put him to death. The battle does not last long. The playing out of desire is seen as acting out within the mythological scenery, but it reveals what had been hidden from one generation to another up until that very moment."[10]

Laius inherited these unresolved griefs, those of his father and grandfather, which he should have integrated before thinking of giving life to the next generation. These ancestors are not truly dead so long as their mourning has not been fulfilled. They are ghosts haunting the living and alienating them. Ancestors have not yet joined the kingdom of the dead and failing to grieve them is sure to attract the curse of the gods. This is undoubtedly the origin of the curse which strikes the Labdacids and which we understand today as unconscious transgenerational heritage. Transgenerational analyses have shown how alienated are the descendants who inherit these unfinished stories. One of the possible consequences is the growth of a drive to kill whoever can serve the transferential necessity as a scapegoat. As long as the original griefs are left unaddressed, individuals would repeatedly want to kill their ancestors' ghosts. This is also the meaning of the words of Tiresias enjoining the Thebans to clarify the circumstances of the disappearance of the former king, Laius, to properly mourn him and allow life to resume its rights in the face of the plague.

---

[10] Cléopâtre Athanassiou, "La lignée de Cadmos", in Revue Française de psychanalyse, tome LVII, avril-juin, 1993, p. 564.

Laius projects this lack of historical integration upon his son and consequently wishes to put him to death. This is not the right solution. Following the rule of the amplification of symptoms with each passing generation, the absence of the father for Labdacus and Laius, as well as the burden of the unmourned deaths, are thus amplified over time to culminate in the infertility of Laius. As Serge Tisseron[11] observes, it appears that what is not said in the first generation tends to become unspeakable in the second generation and then wholly unthinkable for the third generation. This third generation thus inherits problem that can manifest through psychosomatic illness, for example, as it cannot be accessed through language. The following generation is again confronted with it since the original problem replays itself in a way that can lead one to think of it as the persistence of fate. This is surely the way one must understand the parricide and incest of Oedipus, as deeds which reveal the accumulated deficiencies of several generations.

The Transmission of Unresolved Griefs

The influence of unmourned loss in the Labdacids lineage can be observed in dynamics that expel the charge of grief, a process clearly manifest in Laius' chosen strategies. The damage he leaves behind him, the tragedies which he brings, the grieving which he transmits to others, are consequences of his own alienation. This is how we can examine what is at play between Laius, Chrysippus, and Pelops. By bringing on the death of Chrysippus, Laius charges Pelops with the grief of his son, creating a situation that relieves La-

[11] Serge Tisseron et coll., *Le psychisme à l'épreuve des générations : clinique du fantôme*, ouvrage collectif, 1995, Dunod, Paris.

ius from confronting his own mourning (on a provisional basis). In other words, Laius causes Pelops (his replacement father) to suffer from mourning and thus recreates what affected his own father, Labdacus.

The Labdacids Lineage

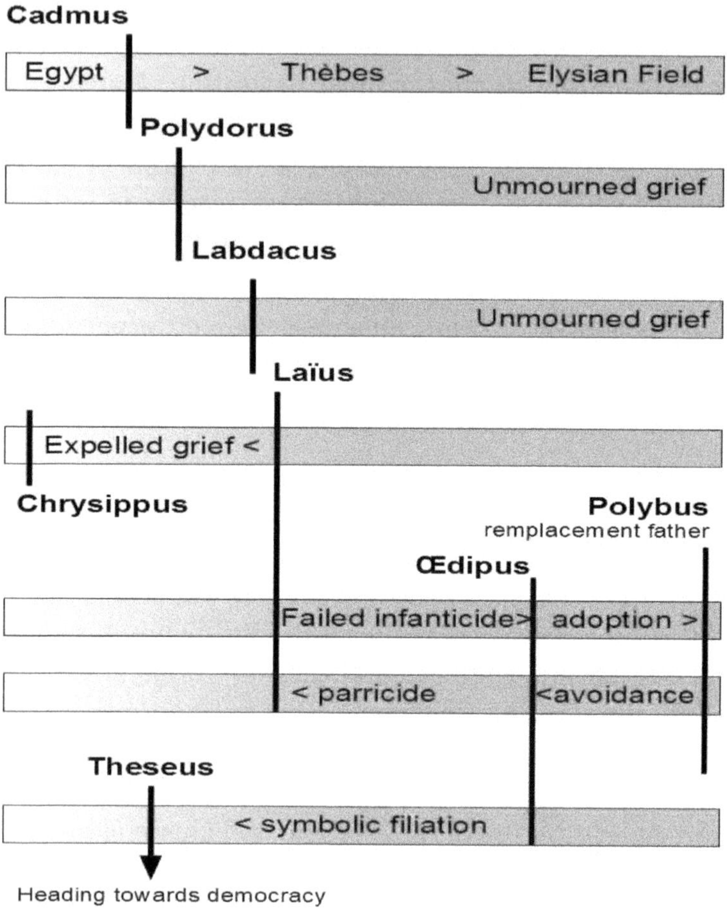

Cadmus

Egypt > Thèbes > Elysian Field

Polydorus

Unmourned grief

Labdacus

Unmourned grief

Laïus

Expelled grief <

Chrysippus

Polybus
remplacement father

Œdipus

Failed infanticide> adoption >

< parricide <avoidance

Theseus

< symbolic filiation

Heading towards democracy

Such a triangulation shows how Laius loaded his surrogate father, Pelops, with the burden of his unconscious heritages. In a sadistic way, Laius managed to transfer upon Pelops the figure of a father in mourning which corresponds to his own experience as a child. Put another way, Laius triggers in Pelops (the replacement father) the suffering borne by his own father, Labdacus. The repetition of this situation signifies that Laius himself has not integrated the death of his father either; simply put, he displaces and delegates the entire problem to Pelops - which is what typically happens in the process of the expulsion of frozen griefs. While this action temporarily relieves Laius of the pain he is unable to go through, this kind of sadistic and perverse approach is doomed to repeat itself while the original problem is still not integrated.

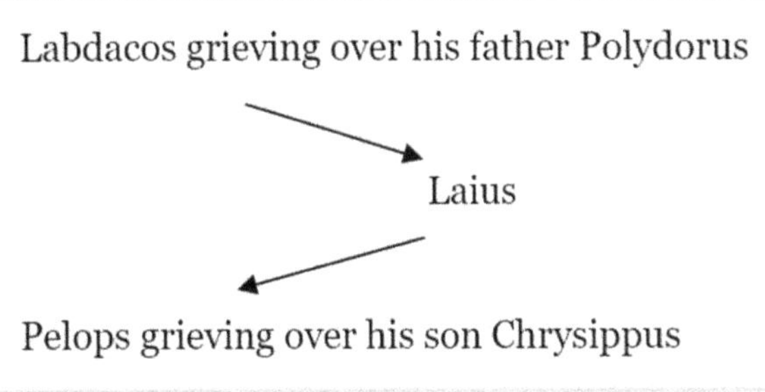

Laius' abuse of Chrysippus, his infertility and his attempted infanticide of Oedipus are all elements that confirm his transmission of unfinished stories he inherited from his ancestors without succeeding in integrating them himself. Oedipus is the ideal victim for Laius to continue to pursue his approach of passing on deficiencies and griefs whose charge continues to increase - a process of transmission which nonetheless has its limits, and that, too, is one of the lessons of Sophocles.

Based on his misinterpretation of the oracle, taken literally, Laius will be able to attribute to his son intentions that hide his problem of sterility. He does not solve and integrate his symptom, but simply transfers it to the child, which is therefore condemned to be stillborn.

Even if it seems resolved with the birth of their son Oedipus, the problem of the infertility of Laius and Jocasta remains. A child is born, but unable to develop as a true Self. In truth, the problem is simply displaced to shape the destiny with which we are familiar. This is a good example of the transgenerational transmission of the problems of infertility that triggered the father's paranoia, his attempted infanticide, and finally the parricide of the son.

As we can see it, this transgenerational perspective challenges the Freudian *Oedipus complex*[12]. But above all, as I have shown in other books, it becomes possible to deepen our understanding of the complex.

We can now understand the nature of Oedipus' transgenerational heritage that comes from the Labdacids. A legacy that brings together all of Laius' lack of integration - concerning unaccomplished grief as well as differences between the genders and the generations - which Laius heaps upon the destiny of his descendant. Incest and the Oedipus parricide then appear more clearly as the tragic staging of such a heritage.

---

[12] See Glossary: the *Oedipus Complex*.

IV

The Heritage of Jocasta

However important it may be, the legacy of Laius cannot disguise the alienations which were also handed down from Jocasta. She too carries around her load of non-integrated events which the tragedy of Oedipus would bring to the fore on stage. As we will see it, Jocasta who manipulates Laius to become pregnant is herself the bearer of unresolved grief, or of a "crypt" to use the terminology employed for this matter in specialized literature.

Her lineage is in effect marked by the tragic death of the first successor to Cadmus on the throne of Thebes, Pentheus. He was the first heir to the throne, but he was massacred by his mother while she was drunk during the famous Bacchanalian feasts on Mount Cithaeron. Under the influence of wine and in a trance, Agave mistook her son Pentheus for a lion. Out of control, she had literally torn him to pieces with her bare hands. On the following day, Agave came back to her senses and was inconsolable.

Johan Jakob Bachofen[1] does not fail to note here Dionysus' irrevocable attitude towards women: "An irreconcilable adversary of the power of women and all the abuses it can cause, Dionysus only grants his absolution to the woman who

---

[1] Johan-Jacob Bachofen, (1938), *Du règne de la mère au patriarcat*, Editions de l'Aire, 1980, Lausanne, p.65.

submits to the laws of the conjugal union, which conforms to its role as mother, and which bows before the superiority of the man and the male."

This grief will never be done, becoming a burden with heavy consequences for all the women in that lineage, down to Antigone. This traumatic infanticide will never be integrated by the Thebans and it will pass down from generation to generation through Jocasta's lineage. This heritage contributes to the onset of various symptomatic manifestations in the Jocasta-Laius couple, for example, infertility[2], the plague which renders infertile the entire kingdom of Oedipus or, yet again, the tragic destiny of Antigone.

An Old Conflict

Before he founded the city of Thebes, Cadmus was looking for his sister Europa who had been carried away by Zeus. Following the advice of Athena, Cadmus gives up this search to raise the new city. After having conquered the guardian of the area, the dragon of Ares, he plants the teeth of this victim in the earth. From this strange seed will spring the first Thebans. Born out of the earth, this native line represents the chthonian forces, the chaotic forces. This lineage contrasts with a second lineage which Cadmus will procreate with the goddess, Harmonia — the line of the Labdacids.

Sprung from Mother Earth, the native-born lineage represents the wild and disorderly forces while that of the Labdacids is said to be of divine order, engendered by she who was the goddess, Harmonia.

---

[2] The unconscious heritage of unfinished grief can provoke infertility.

The Two Lineages of Cadmus

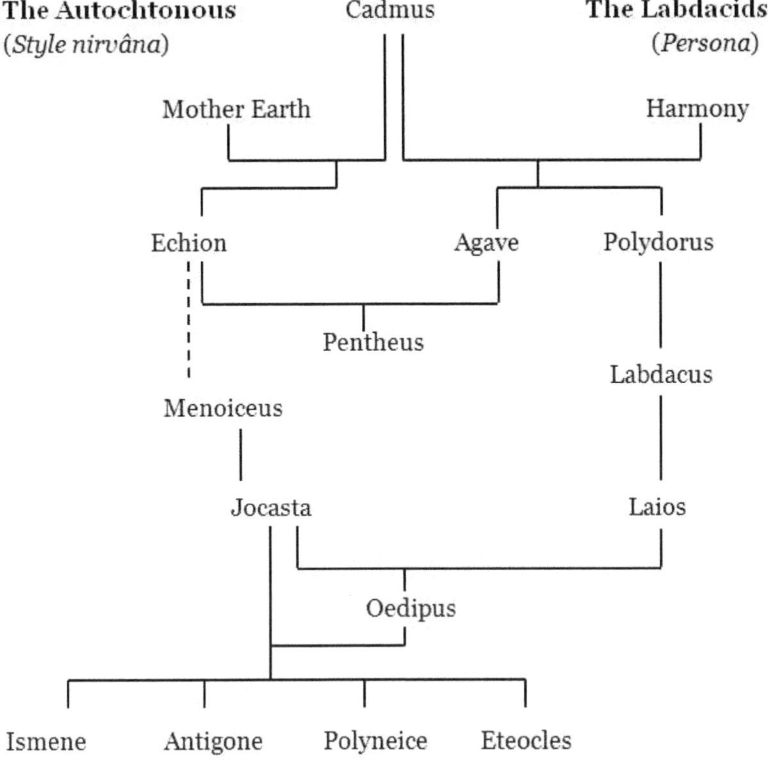

Pentheus was the first to mount the throne of Thebes after Cadmus. He is the son of Echion, one of the men born of the teeth of the dragon sown by Cadmus, and Agave, a daughter of Cadmus and Harmonia. Cadmus thus does not leave the throne to a direct descendant, neither Echion nor Polydorus, but instead to a grandson, Pentheus, whose parents each belong to one of the two lines. However, Pentheus will not hold on to this crown for long. In circumstances which are weighed down with consequences, it will be Polydorus who succeeds Pentheus, and thereafter the Labdacids lineage itself will accede to the leadership of the kingdom. The drama which lies at the start of this transfer of power will haunt the Thebans. Let us see in greater detail in what manner Polydorus recovers the throne from Pentheus.

Euripides tells the story in one of his last plays, *The Phoenician Women*[3] : in a secret place of Mount Cithaeron, Agave, the mother of Pentheus, was celebrating the cult of Dionysus with her sisters. When Pentheus fell from the secret observation spot where he was spying on them, as they were drunk and in a trancelike state, they thought he was a lion and they fell upon their victim to massacre him with their bare hands. Unaware of what they had done, they carried off in triumph the remains of this carnage before they realized the horror of the situation. In truth, Pentheus had been tricked by Dionysus. Without revealing his true identity, Dionysus had proposed to Pentheus to come with him to Mount Cithaeron where the women, subject to his will, were practicing his rites during the famous Bacchanals.

Dionysus in this way took vengeance upon the young king who had not accorded him any privileges since he did not admit his divine origins, although he was indeed the son of Semele, the daughter of Cadmus and Zeus. This intervention by Dionysus in the history of Thebes allowed the Labdacids family to take over the crown of Pentheus. By mounting the throne, Polydorus, the son of Harmonia, established the Labdacids at the head of Thebes to the detriment of the native-born lineage. By placing the children of the goddess Harmonia on the throne, Dionysus sought to reestablish the Olympian authority over Thebes.

---

[3] Euripides, *The Phoenician Women*, 1992, Oxford University Press.

In Greece, those human beings who wanted to rival the gods exposed themselves to the worst treatments. They were explicitly condemned, as is emphasized by one of the replies of the Chorus in the *Bacchae*[4]: "Driven towards your orgies, O Bacchus, by an evil intention and by a criminal fury, and towards those of his mother, with a demented thought and a senseless audacity, he came to win by force an impossible victory. The mortal who possesses a right-thinking mind, who renders homage to the gods and lives following the human conditions, enjoys life without torment. I do not envy wisdom; I rejoice to pursue other paths, great and spectacular which, always leading our life towards the good, towards piety during the day and into the night, make us reject any laws which are contrary to Justice, honoring the gods. May spectacular justice come, may she come with her broadsword to cut his throat from one side to the other and kill the impious man, the villain, unjust and born of the earth, who is the son of Echion!"

The tradition which delegates to the gods the privilege of originating Greek cities is not accommodated by the Egyptian contribution of Cadmus who manages to impregnate Mother Earth. The struggle between the two lineages which results from this will know numerous upsets. Laius, for example, had been obliged at first to leave Thebes because the twins Amphion and Zethos, grandsons of one of the men born of the teeth of the dragon, had seized power in turn. In a way, the sacrifice of Chrysippus, the legitimate heir so to speak, also appears as a factor that reinstalls the Labdacids at the head of Thebes. This scenario essentially corresponds to that which enabled Polydorus to seize the throne, once the designated heir was eliminated.

---

4 Euripides, *The Phoenician Women*, 1992, Oxford University Press.

The Impossible Grief of Pentheus

Pentheus was thus the first victim of this rivalry between the two lines descending from Cadmus. Their conflicts would have multiple repercussions that the history of Thebes would record. Sometimes explicit, sometimes latent, this antagonism furnishes a story outline which in large measure explains the destiny of the Thebans. I will try to keep to the essentials so as not to obscure the main point.

If Polydorus reaches the throne, it will be thanks to the murder of Pentheus by his mother. His coronation involves three generations since it is the massacre of the grandson of Cadmus that will allow the son (Polydorus) to take the place of his father. The Labdacids are not worried about the question of the mourning of Pentheus, which they leave to the care of the rival line. By inheriting the throne, their descendants impose the status quo and perpetuate this unresolved grief of Pentheus for all the other Thebans. And as the proverb reminds us *ill-gotten gains never benefit*. Ascending the throne in these conditions will not fail to affect them also. The situation is generalizing and in the lineage of Labdacids, it will take form with the inability of the sons to mourn their fathers–who died prematurely. Thus, the oracle which announces at the beginning of *Oedipus Rex* that it is necessary to clarify the circumstances of the death of a previous king could just as much refer to the unresolved grief of Pentheus, and not only to that of Laius.

It is thus because of Agave's infanticide that Polydorus took over the throne. According to John Munder Ross[5]: "This filicide was the first that Thebes knew." This drama will leave

---

[5] John Munder Ross, "Oedipus revisited, Laius and the *Laius* complex" in *Psychoanalytic Studies of the Child*, vol. 37, 1982, p. 179-180.

all the women of this lineage, including Jocasta and Antigone, in the turmoil of impossible mourning to integrate. Since then, the relationship with Mother Earth has been bruised at the most intimate of its procreative functions. No doubt, it lays at the origin of Jocasta's sterility, as an alienating inheritance she will replay when, together with Laius, they decide to have Oedipus perish in the same place, on Mount Cithaeron.

The second filicide, at least the second attempt, was that of Laius and Jocasta of Oedipus. Oedipus will secretly survive it, and in the minds of Theban, he will be identified with the ghost of Pentheus. This replacement function can operate because both Pentheus and Oedipus were the victims of infanticide and in the same place, on Mount Cithaeron! The non-integrated story repeated itself, except for one detail, the survival of Oedipus, and this is what makes him a potential hero.

Another parallel with Pentheus, Oedipus was born from a union that brings together the two lineages of Cadmus. Indeed, Jocasta is the descendant of the natives while Laius is the heir of the Labdacids. Jean-Pierre Vernant specifies this filiation: "Jocasta is linked by his filiation to Echion. She is the latter's great-granddaughter who, like Chthonius, represents dark and dark inheritance."[6]

All these elements (infanticide, Mount Cithaeron, reunion of the two lineages) explain why, when he ascends the throne of Thebes, Oedipus embodies the return of Pentheus, the one whose mourning has not yet been done. The transferential necessity[7] that inhabits Jocasta and the Thebans

---

6 Jean-Pierre Vernant, *L'univers, les dieux, les hommes*, 1999, Seuil, Paris, p. 196.

7 *Transferential necessity*, see the glossary.

will find in Oedipus its ideal, that which will temporarily alleviate their lack of integration.

It is therefore not surprising that Oedipus is designated as the one who could save Thebes from the plague epidemic. As ghost-bearer of Pentheus, he conjures for a time all the unfinished griefs in Thebes.

By using Oedipus as the representation of Pentheus' ghost, Jocasta relieves the cause of her infertility. But as for Oedipus, he thus has no other function than to serve as the bearer of a ghost. His true Self has never been considered by his parents.

Antigone's Transgenerational Alienation

Antigone's drama also needs to be associated with Pentheus' unresolved grief. She precisely transgresses the law of Creon who refuses the funeral rituals for her brother Polynices. Antigone claims that these unwritten laws impose the honor of the dead, the first step in the process of mourning. Behind his argument concerning the equality of men before death and the right to provide a funeral, Antigone unconsciously assumes an older necessity which concerns all the unresolved griefs in Thebes, to start with Pentheus.

Is it not Antigone who best expresses the impasse of the Thebans, themselves unaware of the situation? She whose name already designates her as symbolizing bruised fertility: *anti-gonè*. If she transgresses Creon's law, it is to obey other laws, unwritten, sacred, which claim that every human being, once dead, needs to enter history and not be deprived of funerals.

Her conflict with Creon repeats the older one between the native lineage and the Labdacids. Faced with the tragedy that inhabits the feminine line of Thebes since the crowning of the Labdacids after the death of Pentheus, here is what Antigone says: "It is the 'no' of all women that I pronounce, that I scream, that I vomited with that of Ismene and mine,... this 'no' comes from further than me, it is the complaint or the call which comes from the dark history of the women". "It's my body, it's my whole life that screams and often makes me fall. I feel the earth, I bite it, I become the earth and it is its cry that I push". Her words are clear enough as she refers to the unaccomplished grief affecting Mother Earth. She again evokes it when she says she lives for love and not for hate. Perhaps can we recognize here the origin of hysterical symptoms, the etymology of which refers precisely to the matrix or uterus. It is also the indication of an alienating link to Mother Earth. Antigone is possessed by these unfinished stories alienating her despite herself. This is an alienation she expresses in the *nirvana style,*[8] attempting to return to Creon the possible consequences of his decisions.

Jean Bollack also asks himself the question: "Is procreation itself evil?" Should we submit to the Labdacids regime and condemn the children of the earth, these indigenous savages without faith or law? Or share the feminine point of view and avenge the tragic mourning that was inflicted on her when Dionysus led Agave to commit the most paradoxical action that is: killing the fruit of her own fertility.

Let us recall here these words of the Chorus at the beginning of *Oedipus Rex*: "And the City is dying in these numberless deaths. No pity goes to her lying sons on the ground: as no one groans over them they, in turn, bring death". Antigone inherited this other invisible reality. To grieve the dead would

---

[8] Nirvana style, see glossary.

allow an entire community no longer to be haunted by ghosts, overwhelmed by illness. What returns at the beginning of the play is the suffering of Mother Earth for which the Labdacids are responsible. Faced with death, Antigone becomes a spokesperson for the unbearable burden of additional unresolved griefs she inherited from Jocasta's lineage.

The need that drives Antigone is therefore not only dictated by the dramatic death of her brother, Polynices. This event only objectifies her unconscious transgenerational alienations. It carries within it the drama of Agave and the non-integrated history of the Thebans that followed.

Unlike Oedipus, who manages to integrate his heritage in Colonus, Antigone will remain a victim of Theban's unfinished stories which prevent her from becoming truly herself.

V

From Cadmus to Oedipus

The analysis of the unfinished stories of Thebes, inherited and transmitted by Laius and Jocasta, allows us to better understand their influences on the destiny of Thebans. Unintegrated situations and unresolved grief have generated debts whose burden increased with each generation, to the point of programming Oedipus' tragedy.

These first observations on the unconscious dynamic which are passed down in the Labdacids lineage invite us to consider all the history of Thebes. Let us take the time to return to the origins of this city to better understand what links Oedipus to his ancestor Cadmus.

Cadmus the Founder of Thebes

As discussed earlier, on his father's orders, Cadmus left Egypt to try to find his sister, Europa, who had been kidnapped by Zeus. However, on the advice of the oracle, Cadmus abandons the search to build a new city. According to Jean Humbert, the oracle proclaimed that he should follow a heifer to the pasturage where she would stop and where he should build a city. Cadmus encounters the heifer and follows it to the promised land. To celebrate Zeus' granting of this grace, he sends his companions to look for water at the bottom of a cavern which, as it happened, sheltered the guardian of the area. Enraged by their intrusion, the dragon massacres them where they stand. As Jean Humbert[1] explains, worried when he does not see his friends return, "Cadmus dresses in the skin of a lion, takes his lance and his spear, and quickly marches towards the forest. What a spectacle is presented to his view! The enormous serpent was lying on the bodies of his companions, drinking their blood and feeding on their still palpitating flesh. Revolted, Cadmus cries out: "My friends, your death will be avenged, or I shall perish like you!' Straightaway, with a firm hand, Cadmus throws his javelin at the monster, hits him in the spine, crosses his body from side to side, and tears the life out of it. Victorious, he takes the time to consider the immeasurable grandeur of his victim and to enjoy its last convulsions when Pallas Athena, who was protecting the Phoenician hero, descends from Olympus and orders him to plant the teeth of the dragon to obtain in this way a new population. Cadmus obeys the command of the goddess without really understanding it, prepares the earth, and spreads the teeth of the monster in it. Three days later, the clumps of earth start to move, and he first sees spears coming forth, and then plumed helmets, then he sees the shoulders, the chests and the nervous arms of these new men: finally, he sees this strange crop of warriors grow gradually larger."

As soon as they come out of the earth, the warriors start to kill each other off until there are only five left. Echion, who was one of them, makes peace with his brothers, and he em-

[1] Jean Humbert, *Mythologie grecque et romaine*, 1847, Librairie Duprat, Paris, p. 117-118.

braces them and promises his loyalty and fidelity. They become the new companions of Cadmus and are put to work by him building the city which the oracle had instructed him to found, the famous city of Thebes.

This extract of the history of the founding of Thebes renders more understandable what Statius[2] evoked concerning the blood spilled on Theban lands: "Out there, it's the plain, the terrain of Mars, a vast expanse, the fields made fertile by Cadmus. Fearless was the man who first, after these fratricidal wars, these criminal harvests, dared to turn the earth beneath his plowshare again and open up these prairies steeped in blood!"

The creation of Thebes by Cadmus challenges the local tradition. Francis Vian emphasizes it, "Thebes is practically the only non-colonial Greek city which possesses a heroic foundation legend: the other cities attribute to themselves a divine origin and do not otherwise have, strictly speaking, a foundation myth."[3]

If Cadmus breaks with the Greek tradition which delegates to the gods the function of founding cities, it is because he is a stranger as well. Francis Vian[4] remarks that according to Hecataeus of Abdera, "Cadmus, like Danaus, was a foreigner established in Egypt; he was chased out from there with the other foreigners in the era of the Seven Plagues and it is in this way that he came to found Thebes at the same time

---

[2] Statius Publius Papinius, in D. R. Shackleton Bailey (ed. and trans.), Statius 2: Thebaid Books 1-7. Cambridge, Mass.: Harvard University Press, 2003.

[3] Francis Vian, *Les origines de Thèbes, Cadmos et les Spartes*, 1963, Librairie Klincksieck, Paris, p. 231.

[4] Francis Vian, ibid., p. 33.

as Moses led the Jews into Judea." Jean Humbert[5] explains further that "Cadmus was the first to bring to Greece the knowledge of writing and the alphabet, and he introduced to this country the cult of the gods of Egypt and Phoenicia."

Jealous of their privileges, the Olympian gods did not accept the feat of Cadmus which fertilizes Mother Earth and founds a new city. Thus, Cadmus had to serve the Olympian gods for several years for the killing of the guardian dragon. But that did not prevent the intervention of Dionysus who sowed chaos by causing the infanticide of Agave from which Thebes never really recover. In engendering two distinct family lines, that of the native-born or autochthones[6] and that of the Labdacids, Cadmus' city has a fragile ground. The conflict between these two lineages challenges the original unity and its fertile potential.

From Unity to Duality

To preserve this unity, Cadmus had chosen Pentheus as his first successor. Son of Echion, on the side of the native, and of Agave on the side of Labdacids, Pentheus incarnates a synthesis of the two filiations. In other words, his double family bond preserves the balance and the symbolic fertility of Cadmus. On the contrary, when the crown passes into the hands of a descendant belonging exclusively to one of the two family lines, as in the case of Polydorus, the very foundations of the city are called into question.

---

[5] Jean Humbert, *Mythologie grecque et romaine*, 1847, Librairie Duprat, Paris, p. 120.

[6] Definition of the word autochthones according to Petit Robert: "One who is born in the land where he lives, who is understood not to have arrived by migration and not to be there solely in transit."

By maintaining the Labdacids lineage as their leaders, the Thebans were unfaithful to the will of their founder who had designated Pentheus, who came from the two lineages. This betrayal of the creative act of Cadmus will carry serious consequences for the Thebans. By breaking away from their founder, they become incapable of continuing his work. In *The Phoenician Women* of Euripides[7], Cadmus complains of the somber future which is taking shape: “Bacchus has caught you all up in the same disaster, you and him, to consummate my ruin and that of our house [...] - O my child, you the strength of my household, born of my own daughter, you whom the city feared. No one would have dreamed of persecuting me in my old age, seeing you there: otherwise, they would have been punished as they deserved! And now I shall be chased out of the palace, despoiled of my honors, I, Cadmus the Great, the Sower of the Theban race, the reaper of the most beautiful harvest. [...] Now I am no longer myself, but a beggar, and you, a poor unfortunate.”

The Labdacids Complex

As we have seen it, the Labdacids' conquest of the throne benefited from the tragic history of Pentheus and prevents the Theban from mourning it as long as the Labdacids remain in power. We can now analyze how this unintegrated event repeats and expands to form what can be defined as the "Labdacids complex".

Three aspects characterize this “Labdacids Complex”: First, the complex arises from an imbalance between the native-born and the Labdacids (provoked by Dionysus). The second aspect of the Labdacids Complex is that it involves

[7] Euripides, *The Phoenician Women*, 1992, Oxford University Press.

three generations, where the elimination of the latest generation enables the second generation to take the place of the father on the throne. Put another way, the murder of the grandson, Pentheus, allows the enthronement of the son of Cadmus, Polydorus. Third, this complex carries forward the seed of infanticide perpetrated by a member of the second generation on her own descendant.

Even if he does not realize it, as the heir to the throne, Labdacus necessarily carries the burden of the tragic causes which precipitated the transmission of the crown from Pentheus to Polydorus. The transgenerational burden which come with the crown will also mark the destiny of his son, Laius. In passing down from one generation to another, this complex touches the entire Labdacids lineage. As long as the original problem remains unrecognized and unintegrated, the sons cannot accomplish the mourning of their father.

Even if it is transmitted invisibly, seeming to jump a generation as is often the case in transgenerational transmission, we will see that it provides all the elements which lead to Oedipus' tragedy.

So first, Labdacus inherited the problem which made possible the transmission of the Theban throne. In keeping with the law of the amplification[8] of transgenerational alienations, it is in the third generation that the non-integrated complex comes to the surface again with the crime committed by Laius. When Laius tries to get rid of Oedipus, he allows the nature of the alienating factor to be seen: the filicide which was perpetrated upon Pentheus, the event which enables Polydorus to succeed Cadmus on the throne.

---

[8] Proceeding from the unspoken to the unthinkable to committing the deed...

The Transmission of The Labdacids Complex

	Conflit	Latent	Enacted	Enacted	Enacted
Origine	Cadmus				
1st gen.	Polydorus	Polydorus			
2d gen.	Pentheus	Labdacus	Labdacus	Pelops	
3th gen.		Laius	Laius	Laius	Laius
4th gen.			Œdipus	Chrysippus	Œdipus
5th gen.					Eteocle Polynice Antigone

As we have analyzed, the transmission of the throne in the Labdacids lineage will imply, on the one hand, the departure of the father, and, on the other hand, the putting to death of one of his grandsons. In other words, for Laius to inherit from his father, it is necessary first that the father disappear (a condition that is already fulfilled) and, second, that a grandson of Labdacus (Oedipus) be the victim of infanticide, as was the case of Pentheus. Laius' attempt to eliminate Oedipus at birth corresponds to the situation which saw Polydorus mount the throne upon the murder of Pentheus.

After having observed how this complex leads Laius to eliminate Oedipus, let us apply to the father this same unconscious dynamic which supposes that a grandson is put to death so that a son can succeed his father. When Labdacus succeeds Polydorus, the inherited complex contains in germ what is in action in Laius - the murder of Laius by his father Labdacus. Of course, Labdacus does not take action, but the complex is nonetheless active in the unconscious of the various protagonists. With the birth of Oedipus, Laius is caught in the crossfire. On the one hand, as the grandson of Polydorus, he is potentially under threat of filicide when Labdacus succeeds his father. On the other hand, with the possible succession of Oedipus to the throne of Thebes, he finds himself in the position of the father who dies prematurely, as was the case of Polydorus and Labdacus. The accumulation of frozen grief in the Labdacids line increases the probability that non-integrated events will unfold into reality.

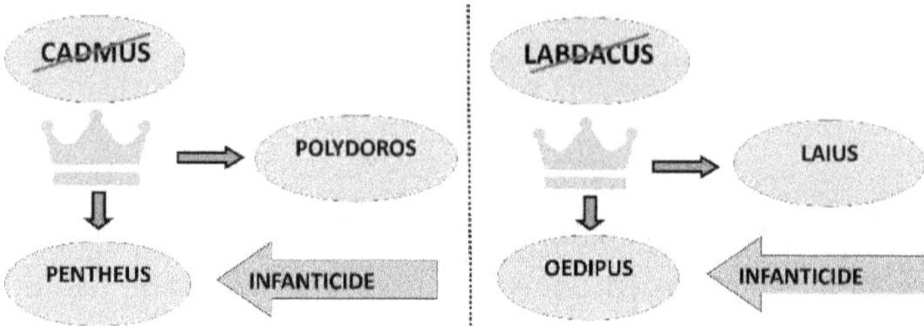

The transgenerational transmission of the Labdacids complex gives meaning to the impossible encounter between the fathers and sons of this line. Thus, we can better understand what, in Laius, condemned him when he meets Oedipus. The very nature of this complex, its original structure, makes coexistence impossible for two representatives of this line. Everything is in place to produce the climax of the Oedipus tragedy.

Some More Wine for Laius

The rivalry between the native-born and the Labdacids reappears for example in the "Dionysian" state of Laius when he conceives Oedipus. It was Jocasta who planned to get Laius drunk to achieve her goals. This episode can be associated with the drunken and entranced Agave during the famous Bacchanals when she committed infanticide. This tragedy still operates in the way Oedipus is conceived, as to replace

Pentheus and host his ghost. Thus, when Jocasta uses wine to get Laius drunk, it is her entire lineage that takes revenge on what had happened to Agave when she had massacred her son under the effect of wine. With a newborn programmed to kill his father, Jocasta reverses the situation, but the original problem remains unintegrated and the conflict will be intensified.

Once again we see that the conditions of Oedipus' conception replay unresolved problematics, which he inherited even before he was born. Thus, we can now better understand why the oracle prevented Laius from having a child. Numerous authors have referred to the part in Euripides' play *The Phoenician Woman* where Jocasta says, "Laius took me as his wife, but since he had no children after having slept with me in his home, he went to question Phoebus about it, and to ask him for male children who would be a part of his household. The god answered him, "Ô fair-haired king of Thebes, be careful not to plant your seed in a fertile trough despite the gods. If you create a son this child will kill you and all your house will be brought down in blood."[9]

For the Thebans, the arrival of Oedipus could have been the opportunity to reconnect with the will of the founding father of Thebes and for restoring the fertile character of their ancestor. For like Pentheus, Oedipus is situated as someone who shares equally in the two lines of Cadmus, except that everything is perverted. These are the consequences of the tragedy of Pentheus which are concentrated on Oedipus and his relationship with the Thebans. Oedipus on the throne is the sign of an ever-present loss and the unfinished grief of Pentheus which returns in the form of the plague.

---

9 Euripides, *The Phoenician Women*, 1992, Oxford University Press.

The Thebans then make use of Oedipus as the scapegoat for their difficulties. Unable to assume their debts, they make Oedipus carry the responsibility for the plague. Paradoxically, this rejection enables Oedipus to free himself from replacing Pentheus. Such an analysis allows us to better understand what is at stake in the exiling of Oedipus at the end of the *Oedipus Rex*. His elevation to the throne hides and compensates the unresolvable grief for Pentheus. In re-establishing the truth about the cause of this calamity, Oedipus discovers himself at the same time that he loses his function as a placebo for the Thebans. To die to this function will be, for Oedipus, the opportunity to be born as himself, liberated from his alienations.

The Parricide

As I have already stated, it appears to be a constant in the Labdacids lineage that the fathers' and sons' paths cross without their ever having lived side by side.

At the beginning of the *Oedipus Rex*, following the advice of the oracle, Oedipus decides to investigate the murder of the former king of Thebes, Laius, to get rid of the plague in the city. When first asked about the identity of the murderer of Laius, Tiresias the seer refuses to speak, disinclined to reveal the truth. But Oedipus pushes him to the limit until finally he reveals that Oedipus himself is the murderer he is looking for[10].

---

[10] "TIRESIAS: None of you knows...and I will never reveal my dreadful secrets, not to say your own.
OEDIPUS: What? You know and you won't tell? You're bent on betraying us, destroying Thebes?
TIRESIAS: I'd rather not cause pain for you or for me... So why this.... useless interrogation? You'll get nothing from me.

Oedipus' parricide brings to light a deeper reality which pre-exists the gesture itself. He kills a father who did not exist since he was unable to give life to a true Self. The parricide is neither deliberate nor premeditated, it objectifies this truth spoken by the oracle and which no one understands. The passage to the act of Oedipus responds to the modalities I defined as *nirvana style*, sending back to the aggressor what the latter had planned to do to him.

For Laius, to meet Oedipus is to come face to face with all the problems he had denied and transferred to his son. The confrontation will reveal the limits of his defensive mechanism. The mere survival of Oedipus is a mortal danger for his father who suddenly finds himself confronted by his unaccomplished griefs, by the reality of sexual differences and generational differences; more than enough realities which surpass his ability to integrate them.

OEDIPUS: Nothing! You, you scum of the earth, you'd enrage the heart of a stone! You won't talk? Nothing moves you? Out with it, once for all!
TIRESIAS: You criticize my temper...unaware of the one you live with, you revile me.
OEDIPUS: Who could restrain his anger hearing you? What outrage – you spurn the city!
TIRESIAS: What will come will come. Even if I shroud it all in silence.
OEDIPUS: What will come? You're bound to tell me that.
TIRESIAS: I will say no more. Do as you like, build your anger to whatever pitch you please, rage your worst.
OEDIPUS: Oh I'll let loose, I have such a fury in me – now I see it all. You helped hatch the plot, you did the work, yes, short of killing him with your own hands – and given eyes I'd say you did the killing single-handed!
TIRESIAS: Is that so! I charge you, then, submit to that decree you just laid down: from this day onward speak to no one, not these citizens, not myself. You are the curse, the corruption of the land!" Sophocles, "Oedipus the King", *in The Three Theban Plays*, Penguin Classics, 1984, New York, p. 177-179.

When Laius orders Oedipus to get out of his way at the crossroads, it is indeed a matter of life and death. For Laius, the point of this encounter consists of pushing away yet again his alienations which he has passed on to his son. For Oedipus, it is a question of survival and of giving himself a chance to become himself. As Marie Balmary has noted, the name Oedipus - meaning swollen feet - does not so much emphasize the wounding of the feet as it does their swelling, a swelling which metaphorically characterizes the whole person of Oedipus because it is the therapeutic reaction of his wounded body, a manifestation of his vitality and his virility. When he defends himself against this aggressor whom he meets at the crossroads, he reacts in the same way as when his feet swelled up to heal an old wound inflicted by the same assailant. Indeed, one ancient version of the myth says that when Laius tried to force his way forward at the crossroads, the horses of his carriage stepped on and wounded the feet of Oedipus, whose reaction was radical and even fatal for his aggressor.

Laius carries within himself the cause of his death, his own demons[11], the same ones which the sacrifice of Oedipus was supposed to appease. The return of Oedipus has the effect of confronting Laius with the unaccomplished mourning handed down through the Labdacids lineage. The mortal danger which threatens him and which he has passed down upon his son is re-actualized by this encounter which reverses the balance of power. Instead of enabling the development of the Self within his son, and therefore acceding to the role of edifying father, and thereby, guaranteeing his place in memory and history, Laius, who opposes the growth of the

---

[11] We will return to the subject of the nature of the wrong which alienates Laius.

new generation, violates the proper functioning of life cycles and renewal celebrated at Eleusis.

The ensuing struggle between the two men puts both to the trial: on the one hand, Laius' desire to rid himself of his failures of integration, and on the other hand, Oedipus' refusals to be the victim thereof. Oedipus' ability to defend himself against Laius signifies that there is a limit to the policy of the transmission of *pathos*[12] which characterizes the line of Labdacids. By refusing to become Laius' victim, Oedipus accomplishes, through his parricide, the first part of the destiny predicted by the oracle.

Even if Oedipus does not act deliberately, but instead after the manner of the *nirvana style*, he is going to overturn Laius' approach by sending the alienations back to their origins - an exploit which is only made possible by the fact that Oedipus himself has not yet emerged as a Self, a reality which will be revealed to him when the time is right. In the meantime, by killing Laius, Oedipus takes upon himself, without being able to understand it, an additional charge which will come back to him tragically at the end of the *Oedipus Rex*. He does not know that he too suffers from the unaccomplished mourning of his father.

Oedipus' Triumph Over the Sphinx

The death of Laius does not mean that Oedipus is finished with the transgenerational burdens from his ancestors, and this will remain the case so long as they have not been integrated at Colonus. Until he is reborn as his true Self, Oedipus still functions in the manner of the *nirvana style* and it is in this way that one must understand his confrontation

[12] *Pathos*, a Greek word which means "suffering, passion".

with the Sphinx at the gates of Thebes. This encounter too has a meaningful relation to the transgenerational heritages of Oedipus, yet another series of tests that he must overcome to get to the truth about his origins. Philippe Réfabert agrees wholeheartedly in the same sense, "The first part of the monster is composed of that part of Laius which has refused any symbolization and which he aspires to transmit without his knowledge. The second part is composed of the homologous part which Jocasta passes on to Oedipus. The liberation of the child, or better, the ability of the child to access the symbolic world passes through the murder of that which, in the parent, refuses any symbolization."[13] One mythological variation claims that the Sphinx was the bastard daughter of Laius, a half-sister to Oedipus. Like Laius, she perpetuates the deficiencies in integration by afflicting her victims with her internal misery.

The characteristics of the Sphinx correspond to the deficiencies which are perpetuated in the Labdacids' lineage. Its monstrous anatomy, a mixture of bestiality, masculinity, and femininity illustrates the dimensions of reality which Laius was incapable of assimilating and which he passed on to his descendants. She incarnates the denial of heterosexuality and exercises a perverse and fascinating power over men who are unable to distinguish between the essence of masculinity and femininity. Oedipus' passionate devotion to the truth allows him to distinguish between the feminine and the masculine as well as between different generations.

With the head of a woman and the body of a lion endowed with the wings of an eagle, the creature terrorized Thebes by devouring all those who could not solve her

[13] Philippe Réfabert, Georg Garner, Claude Dubarry and Lucien Mélèse, *Les Travaux d'Œdipe*, 1997, L'Harmattan, Paris, p. 109.

enigma. The enigma goes as follows: "There walks on this earth a creature with two feet, with four feet, and with three feet, but with a single voice. Alone, it changes its nature among those who traverse the earth, the air, and the sea. But when it walks propped up on most feet, it is then that its limbs have the least force"[14]. Another version of the enigma takes this form: "What is the animal which leaves four footprints in the morning, two in the afternoon, and three in the evening?" Oedipus solves the enigma in a single word: "Man". In effect, in early childhood, man crawls on all fours, then on two feet until he finally uses a cane in old age. Oedipus' correct answer puts an end to the Sphinx who falls from a high cliff.

The victory of Oedipus over the Sphinx constitutes a step along the way to the accomplishment of the oracle's prophecy. What would appear to be an act of heroism only brings him a little closer to his tragedy. From a rational point of view, his response seems adequate, but why then does he find himself trapped, obliged to marry Jocasta when he receives the throne of Thebes as the reward for his victory over the Sphinx?

For Jean-Pierre Vernant, "The human condition involves a temporal order because the succession of ages in the life of each individual must be articulated in the passage of generations, which should be respected and harmonized with to avoid falling back into chaos. "Oedipus guesses the riddle; he is himself a biped, a man with two feet. But his fault, or rather the curse which weighs upon this hobbled lineage, would have it that in guessing the riddle, in bringing together

[14] Euripides, *The Phoenician Women*, 1992, Oxford University Press.

the question and the answer, he returns to the place of own origin, to the throne of his father, to the bed of his mother."[15]

A closer look at his way of solving the enigma reveals that, once again, Oedipus' answer is a defensive reaction to transgenerational influences, still not the action of a true Self in full possession of his means. He only returns the aggression back upon its instigator in what I have been calling the *nirvana style*. His response is a defensive reaction to the transferential necessity[16] of the Sphinx, who herself is a perfect representative of Laius' alienations.

In her description of this episode, Marie Delcourt[17] mentions this point: "The Sphinx asks Oedipus what animal has three feet in the morning, two at noon, and three in the evening. What he has to reply is not at all her name, as is often the case, but is instead his own name, Man. This is very curious. [...]. What is more, one tradition has it that Oedipus had guessed the riddle without meaning to do so. He touched his forehead and the Sphinx took that to mean that he was pointing to himself as the answer to the question. Convinced that she had been defeated, she asked no further and destroyed herself forthwith."

When he discusses this aspect of the myth, Jean-Joseph Goux[18] particularly insists on the importance of this involuntary but healthy part of Oedipus: "It is Oedipus' incredulity which kills the Sphinx. She does not need to be killed in

---

[15]Jean-Pierre Vernant, "Le Tyran boiteux: d'Œdipe à Périandre", in *Œdipe et ses mythes*, Éditions Complexe, Bruxelles, p. 63.
[16] Transferential necessity: see the definition in the Glossary.
[17] Marie Delcourt, *Œdipe ou la légende du conquérant*, 1981, Les Belles Lettres, Paris, p. 144.
[18] Jean-Joseph Goux, *Œdipe philosophe*, 1990, Aubier, Paris, p. 142.

bloody physical combat, like Bellerophon killing the Chimaera or Perseus killing the Medusa, all it takes for her to faint was for Oedipus to withdraw his projective belief in turning the enigma back upon himself, as the source and the sole agent. The simple hand gesture by which Oedipus presents himself (turning the question back upon himself) leads immediately to the disappearance of the monster."

In the eyes of the Sphinx, the self-referential reply of Oedipus should designate himself as masculine and this "Oedipal" response should make the distinction between masculine and feminine. Given the fact that he is masculine gendered, when Oedipus replies to the Sphinx, "Man" or "myself" he involuntarily distinguishes between masculine and feminine. It should be remembered that the only clue to its origins, its name Oedipus, meaning "swollen foot", refers to the body's reaction to an injury to the feet, as for a phallic survival reaction. He could not satisfy parental projections, even before being born, except on the condition of being an uncastrated male. This is his "trademark", the origin of a natural male authority which protects him at the same time as it will force him to have to know himself better. Facing the Sphinx, there is no place for an asexual human. Put another way, it is his primary and uncastrated Oedipal impulse (valid for both sexes) which goes to work and which succeeds to mirror for the Sphinx the disorders that Oedipus already had mirrored for Laius.

The Presence of Cadmus

Beyond the parallels which exist between the figure of Pentheus and Oedipus, the presence of Cadmus seems to be the invisible wire linking these three characters. The qualities of the founder of Thebes appear in his successor, Pentheus, and then in the form of the "positive" alienation of Oedipus. When Oedipus triumphs over the Sphinx, it is the victory of Cadmus over the dragon which seems to be repeated.

Jean-Joseph Goux mentions such an association: "It is further stated that the Sphinx, the terrible monster with furious wings, carried away young people "from the Dircean places", that is to say, from the cavern which was the source of the river Dirce, which was also the dwelling place of "the bloody dragon of Ares", the guardian of the spring, the one which Cadmus killed and whose teeth he planted so that they give birth to an entire army."[19]

From the dragon to the Sphinx the conquest of the Theban land and its fertility is repeated. The stakes are always the same: overcoming one last obstacle before becoming master of the land. Since it involves a repetition of a story, it does not have to take place physically between two bodies[20], the same stakes are found in the form of an enigma–I am tempted to call it a "transgenerational" enigma. The deficiencies of the Thebans which abide in Oedipus, which he manages according to the *nirvana style,* carry with them in this particular case an alienation which seems to weigh in favor

[19] Jean-Joseph Goux (1990), *Œdipe philosophe*, Aubier, Paris, p. 54.
[20] This physical confrontation having taken place between Cadmus and the dragon, while the confrontation between the Sphinx and Œdipus takes place in the form of transgenerational repetition at the level of verbal exchanges.

of the descendant. The invisible presence of Cadmus, in Oedipus, takes on the task of eliminating the Sphinx following the model of his victory over the dragon.

Oedipus triumphs despite himself, just as he commits parricide and incest innocently, without the true Self in him participating. It is therefore not yet the victory of the Self over its alienations, but a simple progression to the heart of the cyclone, towards its rebirth as himself. In this perspective, if Oedipus passes the test of the Sphinx, it is not to liberate the Thebans, but rather to bring upon them an even worse calamity: the plague. The naive joy of the Thebans who think they have solved their problems with this new king demonstrates their superficiality, their estrangement from the truth *Alètheia*. They do not suspect that a wolf has just entered in among the lambs, that they have prepared the arrival of the plague by offering the throne to the murderer of Laius.

The Incest

After he managed to survive the Sphinx's challenge, the rest of Oedipus' journey appears quite logical. Besides being named king of Thebes, he "wins the queen" to reach the core of his transgenerational heritage and the limit of his defensive mechanism (the *nirvana style*).

In *Oedipus Rex*, we find a passage which announces the ending of his symbiosis with the matrix. Despite the torments which come upon him, Oedipus refuses to give in to Jocasta's demand that he give up the pursuit of his investigation of the murder of Laius. His love for the truth is stronger. And how could he escape from the call of his inner Self, this inner force which enables him to survive the encounter with Laius and with the Sphinx? Without knowing it, it is nonetheless in this way that he will free himself from the alienating hold of Jocasta[21]. For Oedipus, desire goes well beyond the possession of the mother: it amounts to an unconditional love of the truth, *Alètheia*, the driver of the evolution that leads his Self to emerge.

What Jocasta expects of Oedipus is that he give up his investigation. This amounts to asking him to give up his development, to give up the rebirth of the Self which is demanding to be reborn whole. And what does she offer in exchange? What solution could maintain the status quo which seems to her to be the better choice? She says that all that desire for truth is only a dream or that they must treat it as such, without worrying about reality. The mythomania of Jocasta is fully displayed here, she who accommodates reality as if it were just a simple mental image, without imagining that it has any relation to the truth. For her, nothing has any meaning beyond what one wishes to give it. "Live at random as best one can, is the best way to live by far. Do not fear the hymen of your mother, many mortals have already shared their mother's bed in their dreams. Those who attach the least importance to this kind of thing are also those who find it easiest to handle life."[22] On account of her inability to interpret ora-

---

[21] The intervention of a so called "providential" castrating father would deprive Œdipus of the relationship to Jocasta and thus of the possibility of integrating his origins. By rendering the integration impossible, the castration of the symbolic incest would stigmatize the maternal alienation instead of freeing him from it. As fruit falls from the tree when it is ripe, Oedipus then separates himself from Jocasta through the birth and development of the self within him.

[22] Ibid., p. 217.

cles–just as Laius could not–she denigrates Tiresias' pronouncements, arguing that "no human creature has ever possessed any gift of prophecy."[23]

Oedipus' journey is not dictated by the deliberate, conscious will to kill his father and marry his mother, but rather by an internal need, unconscious and related to the atrophy of the Self within. In this way, we can better understand why Oedipus prefers to know the truth about these questions which are addressed to him rather than to satisfy Jocasta and preserve their incestuous relationship.

Up to this point, Oedipus, dead in his inner Self, served the needs of the alienations of Jocasta and Laius. In freeing himself from this role, as he did with Laius, Oedipus confronts Jocasta with her transgenerational alienations which she refuses to acknowledge. As she is incapable of integrating them, the shock is too severe for Jocasta. She prefers to die. Consequently, with both of his parents now dead, Oedipus' situation reflects a reality which, up to this point, was invisible–the reality of the Self within him deprived of edifying parents.

To be born despite the plague

For Sophocles, the epidemic which ravages the kingdom at the beginning of *Oedipus Rex* corresponds to parental infertility which prevents the birth of the Self in Oedipus. The invisible heritage (the debt) is brought into view so that it can be experienced and eventually integrated. Oedipus suffers from this situation which was passed down to him even before he was born. It is an invisible reality but one which can

[23] Sophocles, "Œdipus the King", *in The Three Theban Plays*, Penguin Classics, 1984, New York, p. 209.

be read between the lines of Oedipus' speech when he evokes his sufferings: "You are all suffering, this I know; but whatever your pains, there is no one among you who suffers more than I. Your own pains have one object, and only one. Each one suffers for himself and none other. But my heart bemoans Thebes and you and me all together[24]." This empathy for "Thebes, you, and me" signifies a group feeling, which is precisely one of the characteristics of the *nirvana style* which remains dependent upon the fusion with the mother and with Thebes (the mother city in the myth).

This plague which renders infertile all the forms of life represents the charge of the alienations which stand in the way of the birth of the Self. It is the external reflection of Oedipus' internal difficulties, those which he inherited at his birth and which keep his true Self from emerging. Solving the problem of the plague, which is a consequence of the unmourned deaths of the Thebans for their ancestors is a response to his own internal needs. It is also a way of acquiring the means to fulfill the mourning of his own father Laius, a grief that is quite obviously wholly unconscious for him. When he decides to fight the plague, Oedipus relives the experience of his birth but this time he will gain self-knowledge. What is at stake is critically important, far more so than the supposed benefits of incestuous love which are a prison disguised as a paradise for those who idealize it after having repressed it[25].

---

[24] Sophocles, "Œdipus the King", *in The Three Theban Plays*, Penguin Classics, 1984, New York.

[25] To the extent that the ideas arise from the repression of œdipal impulses, as I explain in the Glossary entry on the Oedipus Complex.

The exile

After Jocasta's suicide, Oedipus loses track of human relationships and all that goes with belonging to any collectivity. Nobody could imagine, let alone integrate, the forbidden acts of parricide and incest. It is impossible to find any kind of recognition in the eyes of others. This portion of the myth presents a veritable fetishization of Oedipus, dispossessed of himself. Jean-Pierre Vernant puts it this way: "Thus Oedipus finds himself, cut off from social bonds, cast out from humanity, due to a divine curse which is as gratuitous as the election which benefits other heroes of the legend. He is already a man without a country; he incarnates the image of the outcast. And in his solitude he appears at once to be subhuman, a wild beast, a wild monster, and above and beyond human, the carrier of a formidable religious qualification, like a *daimôn*."[26]

Without knowing it, Oedipus was already bereaved by his father who died under his blows. And his persevering in his quest for the truth renders him indirectly responsible for the suicide of Jocasta. Two bereavements which send Oedipus into the very different world of exile.

Several authors remark that Oedipus becomes the scapegoat of Thebes, the "pharmakos" who satisfies the transferential necessity of the city. Jean-Pierre Vernant analyzes this reversal: "Oedipus is 'twofold' like the pronouncement of the oracle: the 'savior' king whom at the beginning of the play the people as a whole implore as if they were addressing a God

---

[26] Jean-Pierre Vernant, "Ambiguïté et renversement, sur la structure énigmatique d'Œdipe-roi", in *Œdipe et ses mythes*, Éditions Complexe, 1994, Bruxelles, p.28.

who holds in his hands the destiny of the city; but also the abominable pollutant, a monster of impurity, concentrating within himself all the evil, all the sacrilege in the world, who must be hunted down like a *pharmakos*, a scapegoat, so that the city, having been cleansed pure again, may be saved."[27]

As he embodies a double taboo, Oedipus relieves the deficiencies of the Theban people which can now designate him as the scapegoat responsible for their infertility. Furthermore, Oedipus finds himself trapped by his own proclamation, the victim of his condemnation of the murderer of Laius. He is neurotic, divided between the inauthentic discourse which he proclaimed[28] before learning his origins and his rebirth as a Self which is still lacking an interlocutor to

---

[27] Jean-Pierre Vernant, "Œdipe sans complexe", in *Œdipe et ses mythes*, Éditions Complexe, 1994, Bruxelles, p. 17.

[28] "CREON: I will tell you what I heard from the god. Apollo commands us – he was quite clear – "drive the corruption from the land, do not harbor it any longer. It is past all cure, don't nurse it in your soil – root it out!"
OEDIPUS: How can we cleanse ourselves – what rites? What's the source of the trouble?
CREON: Banish the man, or pay back blood with blood. Murder sets the plague-storm on the city.
OEDIPUS: Whose murder? Whose fate does Apollo bring to light?
CREON: Our leader, my lord, was once a man named Laius, before you came and put us straight on course.
OEDIPUS: I know – or so I have heard. I never saw the man myself.
CREON: Well, he was killed, and Apollo commands us now – he could not be more clear, "Pay the killers back – whoever is responsible."[...]
OEDIPUS: I will bring it all to light myself! Apollo is right, and so are you Creon, to turn our attention back to the murderer man. Now you have me to fight for you, you'll all see: I am the land's avenger by all rights, and Apollo's champion too. But not to assist some distant kinsman, no, for my own sake I'll rid us of this corruption. Whoever killed the king may decide to kill me too, with the same violent hand – by avenging Laius I defend myself." Sophocle, "Œdipus the King", in *The Three Theban Plays*, translated by Robert Fagle, Penguin Classics, 1984, New York, p. 164-167.

support its emergence. Oedipus will have to wait until his encounter with Theseus, before liberating this inner Self. Until then, the absence of social contact removes him from those interactions which could facilitate the work of integration. Failing that, he continues to fulfill the function of a fetish for the Theban people.

Oedipus Fetishized by the Thebans

In the eyes of all those who do not distinguish between Oedipus' alienated aspect and his true Self, he is guilty of having violated the taboos–an accusation which Laius leveled against him before he was even born. The Thebans behave in the same way as Laius when they exile not so much the one who has deprived them of their former king, but much rather the one who reveals to them their own deficiencies which he is no longer capable of remedying. Already abandoned by his parents at birth, Oedipus is once again rejected, condemned to exile. But paradoxically, this is also a way for Oedipus to relive that first event of his history to integrate it this time.

Thus, we can say that the relationship between Oedipus and the other members of the community is inverted, perverted[29]. After having been Thebes' savior, he becomes the scapegoat who incarnates the wrong which the Thebans are suffering from and which they project upon his person.

Simultaneously, the revelation of the true identity of Oedipus confronts the Thebans with their unfinished issues - as was the case for Laius and Jocasta. In truth, the Thebans are also the heirs of certain debts which were covered up by their

---

[29] Related to the Latin *pervertere*, “to make turn around”, “to turn upside down”.

recourse to the *king-pharmakoi,* Laius and Oedipus - a deficiency that goes back to Cadmus and the massacre of Pentheus on Mount Cithaeron. For once, Oedipus does not manage to return to the Thebans their failures, as he did for his parents. At least, it will not happen immediately. Only when Oedipus has freed himself from his alienations at Colonus will the Thebans be brought face to face with their failures of integration. Their unfinished griefs will manifest in the fratricidal killing of Eteocles and Polynices, the sons of Oedipus, who repeat the scenario of the mutual massacre of the native people before Cadmus transformed them into the builders of Thebes.

By exiling Oedipus, the Thebans still try to cover up their deficiencies and responsibilities in the death of Laius. But, and this is precisely what Sophocles shows in his second play *Oedipus at Colonus,* these deficiencies will, in the end, be turned back against them. It is Athens (Colonus being a neighboring town) that will benefit from the good deeds of Oedipus. Just as Oedipus turns back upon his father his murderous intentions, he will leave Thebes to her fate and turn a deaf ear to her pleas. The lacking of a father, unrecognized by the Thebans who would rather use Oedipus for remedying them, brings to the context the dynamic from which the fetishization of Oedipus would seem to follow automatically. Was it by chance that in giving Oedipus Jocasta as his wife the Thebans succeed in giving themselves the ideal "scapegoat" with this new king, one who commits both parricide and incest?

The end of this first part of life reiterates the abandonment Oedipus experienced at birth; an event that occurred too early for him to be able to assimilate it at the time. Adoption certainly compensated for this first break, but it did not constitute an integration of condemnation and abandonment by his parents. On the contrary, it camouflages the story of its origin. Nor did it allow Oedipus to be born as a true Self since his adoptive parents had deprived him of truth essential for this purpose. Exile, however, which repeats the first breaking, offers Oedipus a possibility of integrating what previously could not have been. His historical truth "catches his eye" and his act of self-harm is indicative of his ability to become one with the event, to integrate this experience as well as to maintain a certain hold on his destiny.

VI

Oedipus Makes Amends for Family Debts

When Oedipus discovers the true identity of his progenitors, the umbilical cord is exposed to light. As long as it was hidden, it left Oedipus at the mercy of transgenerational alienations which were passed down through both his lineages. But now that the secret has been revealed, he can finally integrate his prehistory and reconnect with the origins.

Because Oedipus was essentially and too exclusively motivated by reason alone, his errors in judgment and the consequences of his false beliefs have led him to his limits. His supposed family ties with Polybius and Merope were the first of his baseless beliefs: a false identity which had procured for him an inauthentic authority serving the secret of his origins and not founded upon the truth. His *nirvana style* expressed his alienation in thinking he was someone other than who he was, a consequence of the secret around his birth. Sophocles criticizes here the culture of secrecy and denial for the debt it generates and its subsequent consequences, like an epidemic of plague.

Paying the Ancestor's Debt

Oedipus must rewrite everything, including his victory over the Sphinx, whose foundations are now destroyed, calling into question once again the legitimacy of his accession to the throne.

His mutilation also betrays his pain at being deceived by Polybius and Merope, whom he had completely trusted. All of his points of reference, built up since his earliest childhood, lose their consistency when he becomes aware of being cheated by his adoptive parents, maybe the worst possible lie. It is Apollo, he says, who is punishing him for having lived in ignorance, an indictment which brings heavy consequences. How can he integrate the sexual dimension - the very source of life - when he was misled regarding his origins, the very identity of his progenitors?

He who tried to fight against the destiny the gods predicted is struck down by a truth which was written beforehand. Like his parents, Oedipus did not know how to interpret the oracle either. It is in this way that we can understand the meaning of the self-mutilation at the end of the first of Sophocles' plays about Oedipus[1]. Not only does it signify the immaturity of Oedipus' inner Self in the face of a reality which he cannot integrate until he has freed himself from the weight of his transgenerational legacies. It also signifies a new awareness, one which is no longer tied to visual appear-

[1] From a symbolic point of view, the obscurity into which Oedipus has been plunged recalls the right of passage in the depths of Mother Earth, a trial which will culminate with Theseus' offer of hospitality which will enable Oedipus to be reintegrated into the community of humankind.

ances, an awareness of another kind of knowledge which likens him to the blind seer Tiresias and which points to greater self-knowledge.

What matters in this tragic confrontation with the truth, the knowledge of the identity of his biological parents, is that Oedipus manages to integrate this event rather than avoiding it as was the case up until this point in the Labdacids lineage. The tragedy of Oedipus then becomes a therapeutic catharsis, a trial of rebirth. I have insisted upon the impact of unmourned deaths in the Labdacids lineage to emphasize the opposite aptitude on the part of Oedipus, for feeling and being able to integrate these events which had deprived Theban society of its connection to its origins, to an edifying paternal figure. This collective missing was temporarily relieved by Oedipus' victory over the Sphinx, and then massively transferred on Jocasta's son, stumbling along, lost, at the mercy of the slightest aggression.

The encounter with Jocasta could permit Oedipus to go beyond the limits which applied to Cadmus. Engendering two rival lineages made it difficult to preserve its original, symbolic and fertile dimension in a rightful balance. Cadmus failed to know how to guarantee the sustainability of his creation. Residing on Greek soil, subject to the regime of a different religious culture, Olympian, from the one which prevailed in Egypt, the conflicts were foreseeable.

On this point, Oedipus takes up the torch and preserves his heritage by choosing Theseus as his heir. To preserve the qualities which Cadmus imported from Egypt on Greek soil, it was necessary to be reborn as a subject and as a hero. Having brought the incest to its end, that is to say, by being reborn, Oedipus condemns himself at the same time as he secures for himself eternal life, the guarantee of a successful transmission. By doing so, he annuls the intervention of Dionysus which led Agave to commit filicide, rendering to the mother the son who had been threatened by the gods. Indeed, Oedipus himself tells Jocasta, "All this would be very well if my mother was no longer alive. But as long as she is alive, you can speak as you want, but, inevitably, I have to fear"[2] as if at this moment he carried inside himself the agonizing memory of Agave's filicide. In this sense, the massacre of Pentheus by his mother, she who herself was possessed by Dionysius, programs Oedipus' incest in advance. The bond between Pentheus and Agave is played out again and even surpassed by Oedipus and Jocasta.

Along the same line of thinking, the oracle which repeatedly announces that Oedipus is going to kill his father and marry his mother can be understood as a reminder of what the gods reproached Cadmus for, to justify the massacre of Pentheus. From the god's point of view, when Cadmus impregnated the earth, the founder of Thebes committed incest with Mother Earth. And to the gods, jealous of their monopoly over fertility, it is the equivalent of parricide when Cadmus substitutes himself for the divine function of procreation. This is why he had to serve the gods for seven years before he regained their good graces and the permission to marry the goddess Harmonia. Equally significant is the oracle's pronouncement that the family will be "destroyed in blood". It also appears to correspond to the time when the native, engendered by Cadmus through planting the teeth of the dragon in the earth, had massacred each other. The destiny of Oedipus will be to realize and make manifest all that

---

[2] Sophocles, "Œdipus the King", *in The Three Theban Plays*, Penguin Classics, 1984, New York.

the divine rulers held against the lineage leading from Cadmus to Pentheus. Oedipus manifests the Theban people's integration failures, all that is repressed, denied and compensated for through submission to a too exclusively Olympian order that abused the other lineage and prevented the mourning of Pentheus to be performed. The myth illustrates the consequences of a policy of repression and denial policy which propagates in a transgenerational way, the very difficulties it seeks to stamp out.

Failing integration, the dramas of the history of Thebes repeat themselves. *Oedipus Rex* finishes with Oedipus' exile, the end of his first life, and one must await the *Oedipus at Colonus* for Sophocles to furnish the keys which enable us to understand the whole of this uncommon life's journey. By the end of his rebirth at Colonus, Oedipus will ultimately surpass his previous condition to become the benefactor of his new hosts. We will see how his encounter with Theseus will play a preponderant role in this reversal and return to a place in collective life.

Cadmus and Sophocles, the Same Struggle?

Now that we better understand the collective transfer which presided over Oedipus' exile, we can engage in the analysis of the work of Sophocles and take up the second play, *Oedipus at Colonus*. It would take the elderly Sophocles close to 15 years to deliver the epilogue to his version of the myth. He was then 90 years old and we are in the year 405 B.C. For André Bonnard[3], "When Sophocles writes *Oedipus*

3 André Bonnard, André Bonnard, *Civilisation grecque*, tome II, 1954, La Guilde du Livre, Lausanne, p. 111.

at Colonus, he has lived beyond the ordinary human longevity: he has thought a great deal about Oedipus, experienced a great deal with Oedipus.[...] *Oedipus at Colonus* is the follow up to the debate between Oedipus and the gods, a follow up made in the light of the myth, but also in the light of the intimate experience which Sophocles had of extreme old age. It seems as if Sophocles, near death, attempts to throw out a bridge, in this tragedy, just a passageway between the human condition and the divine condition. *Oedipus at Colonus* is the sole Greek tragedy which crosses the abyss which separates man from the divinity - Life from Death. It is the story of the death of Oedipus, a death which is not death, but the passage of a man chosen by the gods (why? no one knows) to be a hero."

The subjects which Sophocles treats are quite contemporary for the Athenians. The birth of the democracy which characterizes this era contributes to a great discussion about the role of the gods and religion in the life of men and of the polis. In this debate about the unwritten, divine laws, and those which the new democratic government passed for itself, it is not insignificant to point out the family quarrels which marked the end of Sophocles' life. They present certain similarities with the problems of the succession of Cadmus. As Robert Pignarre[4] mentions, "The last years of Sophocles were saddened by family disputes. He had several children with his legitimate spouse, Nicostrate (Iophon, the eldest, was a mediocre student of his father's dramatic art). A certain Theoris of Sicyone, who came late in his life, gave him a son Ariston, a pale successor to his name and the father of Sophocles the Younger. The heirs of the one bed or the other competed variously in exploiting either the glory or the property

---

[4] Sophocle, *Théâtre complet*, 1964, Garnier-Flammarion, Paris, p.11.

of the old man. They even wanted to put him under tutelage, as having lost his judgment. It was then, if one believes the legend, that he had read before the judges the famous chorus of *Oedipus at Colonus* (v. 668 sqq.)"

It will be to his grandson that Sophocles bequeaths the task of presenting his last tragedy. The parallel with the problem of the succession of Cadmus is striking. Pierre Vidal-Naquet[5] confirms this: "The husband of an Athenian woman and the lover of a Sicyonian woman, he had experienced certain family problems, as his legitimate son Iophon, himself a tragic author, reproached him for having favored his illegitimate son, the poet Sophocles the Younger." A conflict like the one that put the Labdacids in opposition to the native-born would seem to put in opposition the descendants of Sophocles. The designation of a grandson for producing his last work and for assuming the duty of best representing the genius of the great tragedian, is a jump over the generation caught up in the struggles of opposing sides in preference for the generation that comes after. Like Cadmus, Sophocles is trying to preserve, to better hand down, this symbolic fertility which could be lost in partisan struggles.

---

5 Pierre Vidal-Naquet, preface to *the Tragédies*, Sophocles, Gallimard, 1973, Paris, p 8.

VII

Oedipus Reconnects to the Origins

In *Oedipus at Colonus,* Sophocles grants his hero a happy ending. This transformation is made possible thanks to the hospitable welcome of Theseus. This encounter initiates a radical alteration in the way that Oedipus relates to others. Let us analyze what will radically change Oedipus' given condition, starting with the first scene of Sophocles' last work.

Ever since his exile from Thebes, everyone took care to avoid the company of the son of Laius. However, the king of Athens responds to Oedipus' solicitation and commits himself to defend him, if need be. What is it that distinguishes Theseus from the others as the first to finally grant hospitality to Oedipus?

The Encounter with Theseus

As he says, Theseus recognizes his likeness in Oedipus: "I never forget that I myself grew up in exile, a foreigner, like you, and that more than others I have risked my life in many battles in a foreign land. So there is no foreigner like yourself today to whom I can refuse my help. I know too well that I am a man and that I can tell no more than you what may come tomorrow."[1]

George Méautis emphasizes the nobility of Theseus: "It is pure generosity, the pure unselfishness of his character which makes him act, which dictates the first words which he addresses to Oedipus, for generosity and unselfishness are the mark of nobility. He does not yet know what sort of force this blind old man may represent, but promises his support because the man is in exile, because he is in misery, based on no other motive than fraternal sympathy between one man and another."[2]

Beyond his terrible reputation, Theseus recognizes the true Self in Oedipus. In the manner of a psychoanalyst, Theseus recognizes and supports the Self within Oedipus, which asks no more than to be rid of its old skin. This explains why such an encounter will enable Oedipus to overcome the alienation which he inherited from the Thebans and to free himself from it once and for all. At this point Georges Méautis[3] says that Theseus belongs to the same "spiritual family" as Oedipus, that the nobility of their souls places them on the same level, speaking the same language. Their exchange is intense and respectful, the given word is sacred.

If Theseus can recognize the heartbeats of the Oedipus' inner Self, it is also because their respective histories have much in common. Their relations with their fathers were similar in certain ways and diametrically opposed in other aspects. They both receive the throne as a reward for having

---

[1] Sophocles, "Œdipus the King", *in The Three Theban Plays*, Penguin Classics, 1984, New York.
[2] Georges Méautis, *Sophocle, essai sur le héros tragique*, 1957, Albin Michel, Paris, p. 152.
[3] Georges Méautis, Ibid. p. 154.

defended the people: Oedipus in triumphing over the Sphinx, Theseus by returning victorious from the expedition to Minos. Both also played a fatal role in the death of their fathers.

Oedipus, who ignored the identity of Laius and fights his father in legitimate self-defense, was condemned by the Thebans. But for Theseus, the situation was the exact contrary. He had arranged with his father that, upon returning from this dangerous expedition, he would raise a white sail if he were successful. When he saw black sails, Aegeus, thinking that he had lost his son, threw himself from a cliff into the sea (which became the Aegean Sea). Theseus provoked his father's death against his will by forgetting to replace the sails. Although here, the people of Athens pardon Theseus for his responsibility in the death of his father. The citizens of Athens carry him to the throne of his father because of the success of his expedition. While Oedipus functions as a scapegoat in the eyes of the Thebans, the election of Theseus confers upon him a certain immunity and explains in part the welcome which he can offer Oedipus.

There are yet more elements that bring these two men together. Both of their fathers went to consult the oracle about a problem of infertility. However, the resolution of the problem and their attitude toward their sons are quite different. While Oedipus was left in the dark about his origins, Theseus was informed about his dual lineage on his father's side, human and divine. Legend says how his mother, Aethra, was made love to, by Aegeus one night, and then, the following night, by the god of the sea, Poseidon. Moreover, Aegeus left behind his sandals and his sword under a stone, as a sign for his later recognition. When Theseus would be old enough to raise the stone, Aethra would show him the place where he would find the objects which would enable him to be recognized by Aegeus as his heir. This sword, a phallic representation of his father, is the opposite of the fetishization to which Oedipus was subjected. Oedipus had no information about his origins, other than in a symptomatic way, through the swelling of his feet. There again, the pair of sandals which Aegeus left to his son stand in opposition to the suffering which Laius inflicts on his son. By way of contrast with Laius, who was not a father to Oedipus' true Self, Aegeus is an edifying father for Theseus.

Conscious of his origins and strengthened by the symbolic objects of identification he received from his father, Theseus does not need to be reborn to free himself from his alienations as Oedipus was obliged to do. In Theseus, the true Self developed to the point of becoming a renowned hero even before he arrived in Athens. Because Theseus was able to develop as his true Self, he can see in Oedipus another Self like him in spite of his exiled condition. All the grandeur of Athens is to be found in this noble and generous attitude–no wonder he would even be considered the mythical father of democracy.

Before meeting Theseus, Oedipus had never been considered as himself. He was only judged concerning his alienations. Not yet having attained selfhood, but deprived of all social recognition, Oedipus in exile was waiting for the opportunity to free himself from the past. More precisely, Oedipus' true Self awaits someone like Theseus to be willing to take up his extended hand.

Pierre Vidal-Naquet emphasizes the importance of the hospitality which Theseus offers: "Both before and after his 'entry into the city' Oedipus never ceases to be treated as foreigner, and the land which receives him, as a foreign land.

And Theseus proposes to welcome him to the *koinê hestia*, that is to say, into their shared household and into the *prytanée*, the common household of the city, the place where the city welcomes honored guests as well as citizens who are to be honored."[4]

Where Oedipus Recovers the Grace of the Gods

At the beginning of his second play, *Oedipus at Colonus*, Sophocles presents the beginning of the transformation of Oedipus' destiny. He begins with a scene that perfectly sums up the type of relations with others which the presence of Oedipus provokes: a native of the region orders him to get out of the place where he has been sitting. But Oedipus refuses to bend to this sort of order. To those who tell him that this "place is forbidden for any human foot to trod", Oedipus replies that he will no longer leave this corner of the earth. Long ago, during his encounter with Laius, who forbade his passage through the crossroads, Oedipus could not bring himself to obey. At Colonus, this new interpretation can be understood as a sign of recognition of Oedipus' particular status. By becoming the object of this prohibition, Oedipus comes into the light. In any event, isn't he already in this place of taboo, outside of the collective consciousness since the events retold in the *Oedipus Rex*? When the indigene calls him out, is that not an occasion to reconnect with the collective? After having been prohibited from staying in Thebes, could not this new prohibition represent the end of Oedipus' passage through Mother Earth, the other end of his *Via Crucis*?

---

4 Pierre Vidal-Naquet, "Œdipe entre deux cités, essai sur l'Œdipe à Colone", in *Œdipe et ses mythes*, Edition Complexe, 1994, Bruxelles, p. 133.

As he calls Oedipus to leave the place, the local person attributes a particular status to Oedipus. This is the right moment for self-exposure. Upon the act of assuming his destiny, Oedipus takes a decisive step towards emancipation; it was not his fault he had to commit the deeds of which he is accused.

This return among mankind is reminiscent of the rite of passage from the world of childhood to that of adults. Metaphorically speaking, after being separated from their mother, that is to say, once outside the walls of Thebes, the child and Oedipus go through an ordeal combining darkness and the loss of their usual landmarks to emerge transformed, ready to become a member of the community of adults, or citizens of Athenian democracy.

But only the gods could rehabilitate Oedipus. And it is Ismene who recognizes the divine action on the fate of Oedipus: "The gods take you back after having wrecked you out." This return to grace with the gods is nothing other than the reestablishment of the relationship to (divine) origins, so important in all traditional cultures.

Pierre Vidal-Naquet underlines this type of reversal in Sophocles' thought: “Even where, by a brilliant reversal, Sophocles portrayed not separation, but return, in the *Philoctetes* and the *Oedipus at Colonus*, the tragedy of the heroization of the old man in Athens, the separation must have taken place.” This heroic end proves that Oedipus succeeded in integrating his past, that he had amended for the inherited debts to regain the favor of the gods. To receive the divine grace is to reconnect with the source of life, those parental archetypes that are Earth-Mother and Heaven-Father.

Here too we can recognize the extent to which Oedipus is rehabilitated by the gods. The restoration of links to (divine) origins is bearing fruit, re-establishing men in this in-between which is their domain, that is between Earth and Heaven. For Nicos Nicolaïdis too, the final picture testifies to these re-harmonized links: "In my eyes, the key to the occulted mystery is found in the structure of the prayer of Theseus, a particular prayer which must tell the messenger that the king of Athens adores them both in one prayer the Earth and the divine Olympus. By relying on Theseus' reaction, we can imagine that what he saw (whatever the theme of the show) forced him to include in his prayers both the Chthonian and Olympian deities."[5] The conflict between the Chthonian and indigenous forces and the Olympian and Labdacids forces have finally come together to restore the balance between the worlds, a pledge of prosperity.

This reunification of the Chthonian and Olympian forces is part of the Athens tradition since its founder, Crecrops, was himself half-man, half-dragon. Crecrops was also "the first to recognize the descendants by the father and to establish the cult of the father of the gods, Zeus. He was renowned for his educational qualities and for his zeal in pacifying neighborly relations. The mixture of the two traditions, the old Chthonian and the new Olympian, seems here well anchored in customs, since the Athenians say they are indigenous and that they venerate the gods of Olympus, starting with their protector, the goddess Athena."

Oedipus also comments on his metamorphosis: "It is when I am nothing that I truly become a man." To be nothing means here to no longer play a role, to drop the mask of the

---

5 Nicos Nicolaïdis (1980), « Œdipe : le message de la différence », dans *Psychanalyse et culture grecque*, Les Belles Lettres, p.193.

Persona who tries to defend Herself from her alienations. Only then can the true Self be - or emerge. Such a message joins many old and even modern traditions, in therapy as in personal development.

Responding to the Past

The events which will follow in *Oedipus at Colonus* will confirm this perspective. At Colonus, Oedipus will have the opportunity to rewrite his history, which will not take long to appear in the form of Ismene, Creon, and Polynices: his daughter, his brother-in-law, and his son, one after another.

This time, Oedipus has the resources to turn back upon Thebes and its representatives their deficiencies. In this way, he frees himself from a charge which was attributed to him in an abusive way and which he had taken upon himself without realizing the consequences of his actions. While he is giving up his role of scapegoat, those who benefited from it up until now are trying to hold on to the advantages of the status quo. They will nonetheless encounter a different Oedipus who cannot go back now that he has been reintegrated into the community of mankind on account of the generosity of Theseus.

At Thebes, a new rumor is spreading to the effect that it would be beneficial for the city to regain Oedipus' good graces, and possibly to take charge of his corpse. As Jean-Pierre Vernant explains: "The stain he bears, his *àgos*, is nothing but the obverse of the supernatural power which is concentrated in him to lose it: as well as being soiled, he is sacred and holy, *hierôs* and *eusebës*. He will contribute the recompense of great blessings to the city which welcomes him, to the land which will house his corpse."[6] But Ismene has warned her father: the Thebans will pretend to rehabilitate him solely to avoid offending the gods. But their true plan is to bury his corpse at the frontiers of the city, and not on his native soil.

Creon tries to force Oedipus to return to Thebes by reminding him of his faults. Oedipus' reply bursts out: "Unctuous, shameless – where do you think your insults do more damage, my old age or yours? Bloodshed, incest, misery, all your mouth lets fly at me, I have suffered it all, and all against my will! Such was the pleasure of the gods, raging, perhaps, against our race from ages past. But as for me alone - say my unwilling crimes against myself and against my own were payment from the gods for something criminal deep inside me ... no, look hard, you'll find no guilt to accuse me of - I am innocent! Come, tell me: if, by an oracle of the gods, some doom were hanging over my father's head that he should die at the hands of his own son, how, with any justice, could you blame me? I wasn't born yet, no father implanted me, no mother carried me in her womb - I didn't even exist, not then! And if, once I'd come to the world of pain, as come I did, I fell to blows with my father, cut him down in blood–blind to what I was doing, blind to whom I killed - how could you condemn that involuntary act with any sense of justice? And my mother, wretched man, have you no shame? Your own sister! Her marriage - forcing me to talk of that marriage! Oh tell it all, I won't be silent, not now, you and your blasphemous mouth have gone so far. She was my mother, yes, she bore me – oh the horror – I knew nothing, she knew nothing! and once she'd borne me then she bore me children, her disgrace.

---

[6] Jean-Pierre Vernant, "Ambiguïté et renversement, sur la structure énigmatique d'Œdipe-roi", *Ibid*, p. 33.

But at least I know one thing: you slander her and me of your own free will, but I made her my bride against my will; I repeat this to the world against my will. No, I'll not be branded guilty, not in that marriage, not in the murder of my father, all those crimes you heap on me relentlessly, harrowing my heart. One thing, answer me just one thing. If, here and now, a man strode up to kill you, you, you self-righteous—what would you do? Investigate whether the murderer were your father or deal with him straight off? Well I know, as you love your life, you'd pay the killer back, not hunt around for justification. Well that, that was the murderous pass I came to, and the gods led me on, and my father would only bear me out, I know, if he came back to life and met me face-to-face!"[7]

These words were spoken during the meeting with Creon to show to what extent Oedipus has overcome his life story, which seemed to him to be so irreparably ruined at the end of *Oedipus Rex*. It is a question of distinguishing between his alienated life and what truly proceeds from who he truly is, as himself - a difference which he claims for himself, by reproaching Creon for not being able to do so. Creon and the Thebans are incapable of perceiving the dimension of the Self, neither among themselves nor in Oedipus, because they are in effect too alienated by the loss of the symbolic fertility of the founder of their city.

Jean-Pierre Vernant recalls the turnaround of tragic perspectives "When he kills Laius, it is in a state of self-defense against a foreigner who struck the first blow; when he marries Jocasta, it is a marriage without choice which the city of Thebes imposes on a foreigner to put him on the throne, as a reward for his exploit: "To a fatal hymen, to a cursed union,

---

7 Sophocles, "Oedipus at Colonus", *in The Three Theban Plays*, Penguin Classics, 1984, New York, pp. 344-345.

the city-bound me and I knew nothing about it [...] I received this gift which I never should have received from Thebes, after being so useful to them." As Oedipus proclaims it: in committing parricide and incest, neither his person (*sôma*) nor his deeds (*érga*) are at issue; in reality, he himself has done nothing. Or rather, while he was committing a deed, the meaning of his act, without his awareness and without his being responsible at all, reversed itself. Self-defense became a parricide; the marriage meant to sanctify his glory became incest."[8]

After Creon, it is Polynices' turn to stand before this Oedipus who hardly resembles any longer the father whom he had known. When Polynices presents himself, Oedipus seems beyond being influenced. His metamorphosis prevents him from getting involved in the transmission of alienations that Polynices is preparing to play out again in his rivalry with his brother Eteocles. Since Oedipus' true Self has found favor in the eyes of Theseus, he has become another, as he says: "You were born of another; you were not born of me." Such a declaration would appear immoral or unjust for someone who is not living out the transformation which has taken place. To understand it, one must distinguish what pertains to the alienation from what pertains to the Self. Like Creon, Polynices is incapable of perceiving Oedipus as the Self who stands before him, and even less capable of being happy on Oedipus' behalf for the transformation. Thrown into confusion, the men and women who took advantage of Oedipus' function as a scapegoat are willing to do anything to re-establish the old order of things in which he would remain

---

[8] Jean-Pierre Vernant, "Ambiguïté et renversement, sur la structure énigmatique d'Œdipe-roi", in *Œdipe et ses mythes*, Edition Complexe, 1994, Bruxelles, p. 32.

the alienated bearer of the non-integrated difficulties of the history of Thebes. Faced with so much aggression, Oedipus gets carried away in anger as much against his son as against Creon.

Paradoxically, by refusing to give in to his son's demand, Oedipus delivers a more important message: instead of supporting a plan to cultivate the alienation of the Labdacids and permanent rivalry, Oedipus exercises an authority which could serve as a good example to his son and dissuade him from following through with his fatal projects, for it is certainly not in confronting his brother, Eteocles, that Polynices will be going in the right direction. On the contrary, he is only giving in to his alienation for playing out again the fratricidal carnage which took place between the first autochthons of Thebes. This return to the scene of a fratricidal massacre shows to what extent the Thebans have lost the edifying qualities of Cadmus. It was under his direction that the first natives had been transformed into construction workers. His edifying character, as a father and as a king, knew how to transform them from warmongers into future citizens of Thebes. The loss of the edifying qualities of Cadmus is to be observed one last time in the reciprocal massacre of the two sons of Oedipus.

In the end, there is one last factor to consider to appreciate what is at stake in this encounter between Oedipus and Polynices. At the time of Sophocles, the developing democracy of Athens was banishing anything which would look towards a return of the preceding oligarchic regime. The rivalry between the two sons of Oedipus is the opposite of the sharing of power following democratic procedures. How could Oedipus support a monarchic cause, he who had just been welcomed by Theseus, the legendary father of democracy, in a city which allows men's selves the space they need, without offending Theseus, the one who had finally granted him hospitality?

Sophocles contributes to the democratic movement by showing how the citizens could guarantee the future prosperity of Athens, not by cutting themselves off from their roots[9], but by integrating them and restoring the founding qualities of their ancestors, like Oedipus. While the Thebans have lost this relationship to their origins and their inner selves, leaving them subject to sempiternal power struggles, the democratic experiment imagined by the Athenians would grant each person (equally) a place for his true Self. Having integrated his family heritage and his origins, Oedipus is reintegrated into a society with a human face because the society is capable of recognizing and accepting the true Self in each individual.

Oedipus the Guarantor of the Prosperity of Athens

By offering safety and hospitality to Oedipus' true Self, Theseus earns himself a heritage that is far from banal. Several times, Oedipus had told him that his help would be worth a priceless treasure to him. As he offers Theseus his corpse, he explains that the profit which he will derive from it "is worth more than the most beautiful of all bodies." On this point, Pierre-Vidal Naquet considers that Oedipus "is indisputably, even if the word is not proclaimed, an *evergete*[10] of Athens, who makes a gift of his own body, by way of *kerdê*

[9] A theme which I develop in *Sophocle thérapeute, la guérison d'Œdipe à Colone*, Écodition, Genève.

[10] Evergete: a title given by the Greeks to important Egyptian or Syrian kings, signifying a benefactor, according to the Flammarion dictionary.

(benefits). His benevolence, his *eumeneia*, to use a word which belongs to the epigraphic repertoire, is obvious."

Sophocles' message is clear. By welcoming and protecting Oedipus, Theseus becomes his spiritual son, the one who will inherit his benefits thanks to a symbolic transmission that is kept secret. Jean-Joseph Goux[11] analyzes this transmission in terms of a symbolic lineage that replaces the blood lineage. "It is Theseus, the foreign king, and not his children who will receive his heritage, the blessing of his tomb upon Athens. Having been unable to situate himself in a symbolic lineage at the time of his experience of royalty, he finally arrives, after the sacrifice of his vision and long and difficult trials, at a symbolic fatherhood."

Theseus inherits the secret initiatory knowledge which Oedipus grants to him before leaving the surface of the earth. Oedipus explains: "Son of Aegeus, I am therefore going to teach you what treasure you will guard, you and your city, beyond the reach of age and its worries. [...] But this pious mystery which no word has the right to overturn, you will learn, yourself, [...] and, when you reach the end of your life, confide it to the most worthy, so that he, in turn, can reveal it to his successor, and so on. [...] To you, most loved of hosts, to your land, and to all who follow you, I wish you happiness; but in this happiness, do not forget me, though I am dead if you wish for prosperity to remain your lot forever."

At the end of the *Oedipus at Colonus*, Theseus confirms this transmission. He announces the blessing which has already been granted to him and to the Athenians: "Leave off your songs of mourning, my children. There is no cause to

---

[11] Jean-Joseph Goux (1990), *Œdipe philosophe*, Aubier, Paris, p. 196.

moan, as the dead are guaranteed to hold us in favorable regards. They would not be pleased." In Robert Pignarre's translation, we find: "My girls, stop crying; we are not permitted to lament the death of those whose burial is the source of the wellbeing of our land."

One who observed the final scene reports that claps of thunder and bolts of divine lightning called Oedipus towards his death while Theseus covered his eyes as if dazzled by the divine presence. This light which characterizes the end of Oedipus' life is a new reference to the Eleusinian Mysteries which were celebrated by the contemporaries of Sophocles. Georges Méautis notes "that at a certain moment, a blinding light filled the room, obliging the initiates to close their eyes. The very name of this mystery came from the verb *muô*, to close one's eyelids, and that alone shows that this was indeed the key moment of the ritual."

In a way that uninitiated person can't understand, Oedipus departs mysteriously, lifted by the gods or engulfed by the earth - an ending which is not an ending, reminiscent of that of his ancestor, Cadmus. As Francis Vian put it, "A founder is called to receive heroic honors. Cadmus qualified for this, above all others, by his victory over the dragon and his marriage with a goddess." The privilege bestowed upon Cadmus, to go to the Elysian Fields, was shared by Peleus and Menelaus, who also married goddesses. Like them, Oedipus becomes an edifying father and enters the memory of his last hosts and into History.

Oedipus' Integration of His Origins

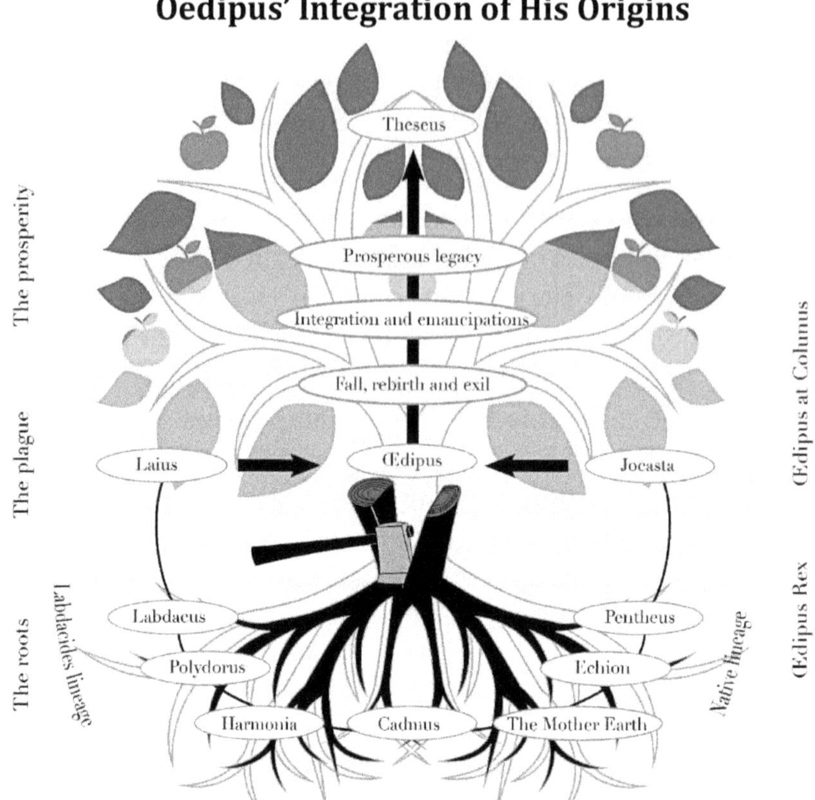

Although it allows us to understand the benefits which originate from the final scene, *Oedipus at Colonus* keeps the secret which was given to Theseus - a knowledge which could not be written down at the risk of being divulged to someone who was not worthy of knowing it. In the manner of the rituals of the ancient mysteries, oral transmission is a privilege reserved to those students who may be able to confront another order of truths (*Alètheia*).

Be that as it may, the prosperity which ends the last work of Sophocles imposes an overall perspective. The two plays form a coherent whole. Starting with the symptom of the plague at Thebes, the central theme of the myth is transformed into a guarantee of prosperity. In the course of this transformation, Sophocles describes the various steps in the rebirth of Oedipus, passing from an alienated existence to that of a true Self which is finally capable of making a fertile transmission of the knowledge which he has gained about himself and others. From the standpoint of transgenerational integration, the restoration of the symbolic fertility of his ancestor, Cadmus, is not unrelated to the prosperity which Oedipus offers to his hosts.

Aletheia, the Un-forgottenness

What forces were guiding Oedipus until he reached Colonus? Oedipus is not just a toy in the hands of unconscious forces. A part of himself is active throughout the unfolding of his destiny, even if he fails in bending it to his will, as he had tried to do. His relationship with the truth is critical here. However alienated he may be, himself victim of his *nirvana style,* Oedipus never abandons his quest for the truth. To discover the truth behind his nightmares, he leaves Corinth to consult the oracle. He holds up a mirror to the truth about Laius, to the Sphinx, and Jocasta. He is ready to make any sacrifice to bring the epidemic of the plague to an end. He even reveals to the city of Thebes the image of a hidden truth, a forgotten truth, that of its unfaithfulness to the wishes of Cadmus the founder.

At the risk of losing one's mind, going beyond taboos, the quest for the truth offers the possibility of rebirth as one's true Self. These are without a doubt Sophocles' most important messages to us. With Oedipus, he shared this love of the pure truth, *Aletheia.* Not a moral truth or historical truth, but a truth which strives for the very dimension of things as they were, as they are, and as they will be. A love devoted to the none forgetfulness of this other dimension of being, as is suggested by the very definition of *Aletheia*, which is composed of "*lethe*" (forgetfulness) and "a" (for its opposite), that is to say, the "not forgotten". Without question, it is the force of the life of the truth itself which brings about the emergence of the Self. The story of Oedipus demonstrates this. Even if he was not aware of the existence of his inner Self, his desire for the truth is rewarded by the action of these powerful life forces which bring about the emergence of his true Self. But the same force was also expressed in the symptoms, that is, the plague, the tragedy at the end of the *Oedipus Rex*, and the crises of hysterical people which enabled Freud to decipher this other reality, invisible, unconscious or even forgotten.

Even when misunderstood, the truth, *Aletheia,* imposes itself forcefully and men must suffer the consequences. And when they succeed in integrating this other truth, unseen by the eyes of the majority of people, then these same forces find a way to express themselves constructively, transforming individuals into their authentic selves and replacing the plague with prosperity. Such a perspective restores to Sophocles' work its *catharsis*[12], its purifying and therapeutic actions.

George Méautis emphasizes the fact that "Without his misfortunes, without his sufferings, Oedipus would have grown old in obscurity among the obscure, and would never have so occupied the imagination of mankind, would never have become, like a hero, the shield of Athens once he knew his origin, once the eye of his soul was opened." As such, it has often been proposed that Oedipus be viewed as the ideal

---

[12] A Greek word signifying the purification of the passions of the spectator when he frees himself from his passion and his anxieties by living through the characters on stage.

philosopher, he who cultivates his love for the truth so much that it gives birth to the subject in himself and leads to self-knowledge, or to "open the eye of his soul" according to the Méautis' phrase.

For the ancient Greeks to live this kind of experience, it means to enter into the valley of *Aletheia*, into a place "where dwell unmoved the principles, the forms, the models of that which has been and of that which will be. All that can be seen and contemplated every ten thousand years by human souls which have lived well."[13] In Plato's *Phaedo* the valley of *Aletheia* is found "above the sky and that these fields provide the nourishment which, as we have known, is suitable for what there is in the most perfect soul: it is that which nourishes the nature of the feathered plumes to which the soul owes its lightness."[14]

Whether it is about opening the eye of the soul or entering the valley of *Aletheia*, access to the truth is essential in the old traditions. The prosperity announced by Sophocles at the end of his very last play also refers to the benefits one can expect from this access to the truth, which is at the root of the emergence of the true Oedipus, as himself.

---

13 Marcel Detienne, *Les Maîtres de Vérité dans la Grèce archaïque*, 2006, Librairie Générale Française, Paris, p. 212.
14 Plato, *Complete Works*. Hackett, 1997.

Conclusion

The preceding analyses have allowed us to better understand the teaching underlying Sophocles' plays. The transgenerational principles, which until now have remained in the shadows, provided Sophocles with the invisible architecture that gives strength and coherence to his version of the myth of Oedipus. With History as the sole judge, the durability of his work testifies to the relevance of the ancient wisdoms that he had made his own and that guided his pen.

To shed light on Sophocles' knowledge, I have proposed a transgenerational interpretation that respects the symbolic dimension of the myth. From this viewpoint, the alienation of Oedipus, his tragedy, his rebirth as a Self, and finally his emancipation at Colonus, are integrated into a global perspective. From Thebes to Colonus, Oedipus' journey is as much an illustration of the tragic spectacle of transgenerational alienation as it is an illustration of its healing.

Beyond the tragedy, Sophocles invites us to understand Oedipus' metamorphosis. Alienated by his transgenerational legacies when he was King of Thebes, Oedipus illustrates a lack of roots, a superficial life composed of mere appearances, too rational. Although the status of being a king may seem an ideal state, it is no protection against the consequences of a lack of self-knowledge. By dramatizing the situation Sophocles shares a valuable message with his time and with ours. He thus encourages us to take into account the unwritten laws that govern transgenerational transmission, the way in which they can alienate us, and the role of the Self, capable of integrating these legacies.

To understand the real causes of the plague described by Sophocles at the beginning of *Oedipus the King* we had to return to the origins of Thebes. By threatening to destroy everything which Cadmus had built, the plague required the Thebans to rediscover the edifying character of the founder of Thebes.

As we have seen, the original qualities of Cadmus were lost the moment Polydorus took the throne after the massacre of Pentheus by his own mother. From that time on, the history of Thebes would be nothing more than a series of conflicts between the native people and the Labdacids. By overturning the balance of forces that were part of Thebes' origin, the intervention of Dionysus engenders the *Labdacids Complex* which alienates the Thebans and reaches its climax in the tragedy of Oedipus.

Once he establishes himself on the throne of Thebes, Oedipus takes upon himself the burden of the unresolved issues in the history of the city. This burden is too heavy for Oedipus, who himself is already alienated without knowing it. His investigation of the causes of the plague will nonetheless allow him to discover his true origin. Thus, he can be reborn as his true Self, which will enable him to rewrite his prehistory and to free himself from it. Ultimately, he reconnects with the potential fertility of Cadmus. Oedipus becomes the inheritor of the same edifying character which belonged to Cadmus, his ancestor, as the guarantor of prosperity. He hands down these virtues to Theseus because he is the only one who has shown he is worthy of inheriting this secret knowledge.

This proposed transgenerational interpretation has advanced in stages. By associating elements that were originally dispersed in the history of Thebes, I tried to bring together their meaning to a common perspective. Such an approach is similar to the work of transgenerational integration which progressively reconstitutes the meaning of certain experiences that would otherwise be difficult to integrate.

I could have presented this transgenerational analysis starting from the loss of Cadmus' edifying qualities as a founder and in showing how this loss has repercussions down to the tragedy of Oedipus. But it seemed to me that it would be more rewarding to allow the reader to experience in the reading itself the unfolding of an analysis which begins with open questions rather than for me to supply the elements of the answers too summarily. Starting with an actual and visible problem (the plague) the first ideas give way to the unexpected. The invisible makes its way out of the shadows until the entire psycho-genealogical structure of the Oedipus myth appears in our view. Everything is already there, present, from the first glance. The words which lead us to believe in a return to the past are deceptive because it is not so much a question of going back in time as it is a matter of making apparent the unfinished past which is still present, hidden behind appearances. Healing is made possible by considering the difference between one's true Self and the part of oneself which is alienated by transgenerational legacies.

A Longstanding Tradition

As I have developed in a previous book[90], we must remember that Sophocles was a multi-talented man and it is

---

90 *Sophocle thérapeute*, Genesis Editions, Geneva.

worth noting that he served as a priest of Asclepius, supporting the entry of this healing god into Athens. Sophocles' knowledge as a "healer" is evident in the therapeutic transformation of Oedipus at Colonus. The sources of this healing tradition are Egyptian and hermeneutic. A lineage that starts with Thot-Hermes, the inventor of writing, and continues with Hermes Trismegistus, the scribe of the gods, and with Asclepius, the healer who would be beatified and venerated under the name Aesculap[91] by the Romans. The legend had it that whoever could decipher the magic formulas of the *Book of Thot* could surpass the gods. Cadmus was specifically regarded as the one who brought writing to Greece, as well as other aspects of Egyptian traditions. Referring to the Egyptian god, Thot, the edifying qualities of Cadmus would provoke the jealousy of the Greek gods and the decisive intervention of Dionysus.

In ancient traditions, the procedures for regeneration and rebirth were manifold. To begin with, there is the rebirth of Osiris, who is then venerated by all the Egyptians as the very symbol of the guarantee of the renewal of life. In the *Corpus Hermeticum,* the metaphor of the crater is the same as the challenge of the truth which allows Oedipus to be reborn: "You who can dive into this crater here, you who believe that you will rise again towards He who has set this crater upon the earth, you who know why you have come into being."[92] Finally, how can one avoid relating Oedipus' rebirth to the rites of passage practiced in ancient times to effectuate the transformation of children into adults? The different

[91] Just as the Greeks introduced Asclepius into Athens to fight against the plague, so the Romans would import him for the same reason.
[92] Hermès Trismégiste, *Corpus Hermeticum*, tome 1, 2011, Les Belles Lettres, Paris, p. 50.

steps in such a trial can be recognized in Sophocles' version of the myth of Oedipus. After his journey to the origins (incest), Oedipus reconnects with the community at Colonus.

With one foot in the ancient traditions in decline and one foot in the rise of rational philosophy and the democratic project in Athens, Sophocles brings together and transcends the two worlds. Like the cult of the *Eleusinian Mysteries* near Athens, whose origin was Egyptian as well, Sophocles' work is faithful to the ancient traditions. Like a window which opens upon another reality, Sophocles' myth of Oedipus immortalizes the ancient traditions in a "democratic" form, that is to say in a form not solely reserved to devotees, but accessible to the greatest number of people with the tragic Greek theatre. Created in this transitional period, at the dawn of modern civilization, Sophocles makes it possible to establish a dialogue between several realities. His tragedies fulfill the same function as the renowned *Rosetta Stone* on which the same text was written in three different languages. Both the *Rosetta Stone* and the plays of Sophocles enable us to decipher and understand ancient knowledge.

A New Paradigm for Today

It goes without saying that this new interpretation of the myth of Oedipus challenges all previous discussions and reopens many questions hitherto left open – some of which I have analyzed in my other books. As I proposed to understand it in the introduction, if Freud and the psychoanalysts, Lévi-Strauss, Pasolini, Voltaire, academics and Hellenists and so many others have failed to solve the enigma that the works of Sophocles constituted for them, it is because they lacked the main key: the awareness of transgenerational legacies and their weight on the destiny of humankind, which we have rediscovered thanks to contemporary therapeutic practices and epigenetic research.

This ignorance of transgenerational dynamics does not exempt us from the consequences of transgenerational legacy. On the contrary, so long as they remain unconscious, transgenerational legacies can freely develop their alienating powers on individuals and collectivities. Thus, in parallel to this new understanding of the Oedipus myth, transgenerational analysis can also resolve many other problems whose nature and origin have not been yet examined.

With his version of the story of Oedipus, Sophocles leaves us with a universal model of therapy that can serve as a reference. In addition to inspiring men and women writers, artists and cultural actors, his universal model of therapy provides a valuable frame of reference for transgenerational therapies[93], parent/child relations, infertility issues, personalized medicine, the use of DNA testing, psychogenetics, perspective on migration-related issues, and as a support for genealogical research.

Indeed, the lessons from this model are numerous. In the first place, we must remember the importance of incomplete mourning, the consequences of which have repercussions on several generations, and which manifested themselves in the infertility of Laius and Jocasta.

But beyond these rather explicit parallels, this new interpretation of the myth takes us back to the roots of our civilization to better measure what has been lost to us from ancient knowledge. It is a matter of recalling the importance of unwritten laws, the laws of life, contrary to which modern

---

93 See my recent book: *Transgenerational Therapy and Psychogenetics*, Genesis editions, 2020, Geneva.

civilization has preferred to oppose its own laws, those written by humans, a development that redefines human nature. Initially considered as children of Nature and Mother Earth, integrated into a whole, individuals have become citizens cut off from the earth, children of the city, structured by the laws of the society written by its leaders. On its face, this is a change that would allow citizens to enjoy equal rights in a more democratic project. This change, however, has simultaneously deflected us away from origins, causing a deep wound which is the cause of many of our current problems.

In *Civilization and Its Discontents*, Freud recognized the problems that follow this severing of the link to the origins with the repression of the oedipal problem. "The tendency of culture to set restrictions upon sexual life is no less evident than its other aim of widening its sphere of operations. Even the earliest phase of it, the totemic, brought in its train the prohibition against incestuous object-choice, perhaps the most maiming wound ever inflicted throughout the ages on the erotic life of man. Further limitations are laid on it by taboos, laws, and customs, which touch men as well as women."[94] As I have tried to show, although he did manage to identify the issue, Freud's analysis perfectly illustrates the prejudices of our modern civilization and its ignorance of the - more essential - need to integrate transgenerational legacies in order to become a true Self. Deprived of its symbolic meaning, and of the second part of the story, *Oedipus at Colonus*, the myth is dramatized in modern civilization, which has cut itself off from its origins.

---

94 Sigmund Freud, *Civilization and Its Discontents* (J. Riviere), 1930, The Hogarth Press, Chapter IV.

Freud was nevertheless able to recognize the original problem of the discontent in our civilization that we can analyze today in a different way. By misunderstanding these unwritten and transgenerational laws, instead of integrating our links with our origins as well as our transgenerational legacies, as advocated in traditional cultures, our modern civilization will have repressed them by means of its new written laws at the same time as it represses the Oedipal complex. As a result, our entire relationship to the world that gave us birth is affected, as if it were a forbidden love relationship. This is a world that does not stop at the mere representation of the mother, but includes family lines and the whole world (i.e. our origins), of which we are an emanation and from which we cannot cut ourselves off without perishing.

However ethical they may seem, the laws written by men and woman will nevertheless continue to cause this deep wound to repress our link to origins and love for the sources of life. It is precisely here that the transgenerational interpretation of the myth of Oedipus offers us to recapture the original problem differently. This alternative which takes back the symbolic dimension of the *psyche* to its original conflict and provides another solution, that of an integration of these most archaic links. An integration made possible by considering transgenerational legacies and restoring the original fertility, i.e. the perspective of prosperity that ends *Oedipus at Colonus*.

We can now better understand why, in our modern civilization, the link to Mother Earth has remained dependent on an Oedipal complex that biases relationship between generations. Under the pretext of incest, as well as under the threat of a tragedy that would be insurmountable (the one that punctures *Oedipus the King*), the links between generations are being tainted, carrying alienations rather than the vectors of an edifying transmission. Yet the transgenerational re-reading of the Oedipus trilogy teaches us to what extent we have missed the essential transgenerational point. In its symbolical meaning, the story is in no way about incest or a so-called return to the original matrix, but rather about the way out of the matrix of a Being who was not yet born as a true Self.

Instead of focusing on a forbidden access to Mother Earth and cultivation of a conflicted relationship, by seeking to exploit it, for example, we would do better to reappropriate our origins and integrate them. And instead of trying to cut the "umbilical cord", perhaps the most symptomatic fantasy of our modern civilization, we should integrate it on a symbolic level in order to preserve our relationship with the forces of the living world of which we are the product.

As a new branch of the tree could not develop by cutting itself off from its trunk and roots, we cannot exist independent of the world around us, of which we are an emanation. We are the fruits of an extraordinary evolution, spanning millions of years, from which we imagined we could dissociate ourselves, just as we had imagined we could dissociate ourselves from our parents and ancestors. Once we have integrated our belonging to the environment that gave birth to us, and once we have recognized that is it still part of what constitutes and nourishes us, we would not need additional repressive laws that would supposedly prevent us from continuing to harm (pollute and instrumentalize) nature (Mother-Earth). Instead of giving the superego discourse full rein introducing new laws, with their repressive measures and without in any way guaranteeing the necessary consciousness, the aim should be to succeed in passing on to future generations the awareness of the importance of our links to our origins, which implies the transmission of family and collective history, and even the integration of our transgenerational legacies. Peter Sloterdijk also points out: "The social sciences and humanities of today are gradually becoming aware that fundamental concepts that had been considered to have been thought through to the end, such as generation, filiation and inheritance, had never been taken into consideration by them with the seriousness required by the abysmal nature of the topic."[95]

Sophocles wrote his plays in reference to the plague that ravaged Athens between 430 and 426 BC. Among the many victims was the famous Pericles, the charismatic and emblematic leader of ancient Athenian glory, who was suspected of having inherited a family curse. With his version of the story of Oedipus, Sophocles takes up these themes to offer his fellow citizens a therapeutic model capable of preserving them from a repetition of history. This model sheds light on traumatic events to allow men and women to integrate them, the first antidote to the risk of seeing them repeated. This is the traditional role of the great minds of that time, guides of the collective consciousness, each in their own way, dealing with the most fundamental problems. Symbolic and universal, Sophocles' model remains as relevant today as it was in his own time - assuming that, like Theseus and his people in the legend, we would deserve this legacy.

With climate crisis and viral pandemics, we are confronted with these laws of life elude by us, as if they were

---

95 Peter Sloterdijk (2018), *Après nous le déluge, les temps modernes comme expérience antigénéalogique*, Payot, Paris. [*After us, the deluge, modern times as an anti-genealogical experience*.]

catching up to us after we have constantly interposed our own written and economic laws on them. With his therapeutic model, Sophocles proposes we take the example of Oedipus who restores his links to the multiple forces of the living, that is to say, to the origins. The new transgenerational interpretation of the Oedipus myth has brought to light this alternative path of integrating our links to origins. This path would be synonymous with prosperity, while that of severing these links, or of their instrumentalization, would be tantamount to inviting the direst of calamities.

Recognizing and appropriating Sophocles' teaching can help us to regain sight of the unwritten laws that govern the destiny of men and women. For that reason, I felt it was of overarching importance to share this new transgenerational interpretation of the myth of Oedipus and illustrate how Sophocles was able to stage his knowledge of transgenerational laws. To remediate our relationship with our origins and to preserve future generations, or at least to give them the means to integrate their experiences, the therapeutic model left to us by Sophocles deserves to be finally acknowledged today.

Glossary

Alienation
Integration
Transferential Necessity
Fetishism
The Nirvana Style
The Persona and the divided *Persona*
Oedipus Complex
Self-Knowledge

Alienation

The verb "to alienate"[1] appears in the law (1265) as a borrowing from the Latin *alienare*, "to render another" or "to render a stranger", derived from *alienus*, "other", itself and from *alius* (elsewhere, alias, alibi). After the old Provencal *aliénât*, "to alienate" becomes more defined in the 13th century, with the mean of "drive someone crazy". From which comes "aliéné", more common in the 14th century as a replacement for "crazy" in institutional jargon.

In the 20th century, the word alienation (then aliéner, aliénant in 1943, by Sartre) took on a new usage, being chosen as the translation of the German *Entfremdung*, an important philosophical concept for Hegel, and then for Marx, "the state where a human being seems detached from himself, turned away from his true awareness by socio-economic

[1] From the dictionary of the "History of the French language", *Le Robert*, Paris, p. 45.

conditions." The success of this concept led to the use of the word and certain derivatives (aliénant, aliénateur) in a more vague sense: "a human being's loss of authenticity", bringing together the 18th century's popular theme of the harmful effects of life in society and the 19th century's theme of the exploitation of man by man.

Integration

Integration[2] is a psychological function which corresponds to the general idea of a process of assimilation, of "digestion", something which we do naturally as we try to understand and make sense of what we have experienced. By integrating our relationship with the world, we perform a psychological chore that responds to the healthy and natural need to make sense of life. Integration is an essential psychological function that allows one to enter one's experiences into history, to truly relegate the past to the past, to liberate the mind for enhanced thinking about daily life.

Thus, integration is a process of psychological assimilation of daily experiences. Whatever is not integrated, or is not sufficiently integrated, becomes a source of difficulty for one's true Self or others. It is essential for each person to assimilate his or her experience in his or her unique way, and to be able to enter it meaningfully into what constitutes that person's history. Otherwise, the events, which are psychologically suspended instead of integrated, not only repeat themselves and perpetuate their existence throughout life but even worse, they pass down their pathological burden to succeed-

[2] Excerpts from "*Rooted in the Present, The Emergence of the Self*", Ecodition, 2014, Geneva.

ing generations. In the model which pertains to the patriarchal system, the repression of the *Oedipus Complex* postpones the achievement of its integration for all eternity.

The purpose of therapy is to facilitate the possibility of integration where it is lacking, in personal history as well as in family and cultural history. One's true Self plays a key role in this work. It is the guarantor of a genuine integration of the most profound aspects of its existence.

Integration is derived from Nicolas Abraham and Maria Torok's idea of "introjection". For these authors, introjection is a conscious appropriation, with or without the help of a therapeutic method, of zones of the psyche which are rejected, repressed, anonymous, misunderstood, divided or dead. "In general, we can consider that the affirmative definition of the process of introjection is the creation of the Self through encountering novelty."[3]

Finally, if we draw inspiration from the teachings of Sophocles, it appears that the Self occupies a central role in this function of integration. It is the true Self that integrates an individual's history, and that is why Oedipus must first be reborn as this Self before he can liberate himself from his past. Integration is thus a work of introjection performed by the Self. And so, transgenerational integration refers to the work of one's true Self which rewrites its prehistory at the same time as it evolves.

---

3 Nicholas Rand, *Quelle psychanalyse pour demain*, 2001, Érès, Paris, p. 38.

Transferential Necessity

Transferential Necessity[4] describes a dynamic substitute for integration. Whereas integration transforms the psychological past into a symbolic past, transferential necessity goes no further than to maintain the non-integrated elements outside of one's Self. This psychological repressive policy merely postpones and perpetuates the same conflictual dynamics in the destiny of the person. Transferential necessity is a defensive reaction for those who are not capable of completing the work of assimilation which requires "cogitation" and symbolic elaborations, which are the prerequisites for performing any integration. Otherwise, for whatever reason, a relationship of detachment from one's true Self, a sort of psychological block sets in, such as denial or repression. By maintaining the experience outside of the Self, this lack of integration is frozen in a transfer towards a particular aspect of the world. In a relationship of detachment from oneself, the non-integrated elements crystallize in the external world. In parallel with the alienation which is a division between one's Self and the rest of the person, the non-integrated experiences persist outside of the Self, in the body, transferred onto others or the world as a whole. In the latter case, it contributes its characteristics to one's *Weltanschauung* (or "world view").

What is important about this concept of "transferential necessity" is that it takes into account the persistent existence outside of the Self of a conflict related to a particular experience. Nothing is integrated. The problem is duplicated, transposed on another aspect of reality, which is thereupon

---

[4] Excerpts from "*Rooted in the Present, The Emergence of the Self*", Ecodition, 2014, Geneva.

experienced as problematic. Transferential necessity is none other than psychoanalytic transference doubled by the need which arises from the lack of integration. Sigmund Freud has demonstrated how the transfer repeats a past event in the present. One's difficulty with integrating problematic events is definitively proportional to the absence of one's inner Self. It is this inner Self that integrates experiences whereas the ego desperately tries to get rid of them by projecting them outside of itself.

From a transgenerational perspective, the impossibility of integrating an unconscious legacy translates into a tendency to project the charge of this legacy onto the next generation. By way of contrast, by developing the role of the Self, like Oedipus, the chain of transmission is purged of the symptomatic charges so that it becomes symbolic, edifying, and even the guarantor of prosperity.

Fetishism

Fetishism is a very profound (archaic) psychological alienation whose cause is traditionally attributed to overwhelming castration anxiety experienced in infancy. Fetishism results from a restructuring of the psyche which follows upon the aggravation of the Oedipal problem, in which the anxiety about castration is "resolved" employing a lie that denies reality. To suppress this anxiety, the fetishist transfers to another object the property of being the penis of the female sex organs. The fetishist sees the female penis in the fetish object, the foot for example. Thus, both sexes have a penis, which allows the fetishist to preserve the infantile belief that there is no difference between the sexes, and thus no reason to be anxious about a possible castration.

From a transgenerational perspective, rather than attribute the origin of this anxiety to the infant, we interpret it as the sign of a lack of integration of sexual differences which unconsciously affects one or both of the parents. The unresolved issue, repressed by the adult, manifests itself in the infant through castration anxiety when he is himself confronted with the gender difference. The child experiences anxiety in an amplified way since it was repressed, instead of integrated, by the adult.

The Nirvana Style

The concept of the *nirvana style*[5] allows us to understand the meaning of certain behaviors, with no apparent meaning, which are characterized, however, by a very specific style. They translate into action something which would not belong to the person himself, but which exists in an interpersonal collective space. This plural, interpersonal space is also that through which the transgenerational legacies are transmitted. In general, by the *nirvana style*, I mean those behaviors which are induced by a lack of integration, put into action by the descendants as part of his transgenerational alienation. The behaviors which pertain to the *nirvana style* are symbolic by nature, they form a language for which words are lacking, they speak of certain experiences whose symbolization has been degraded to the point of losing any language but the dramatic.

Resorting to the *nirvana style* is evidence of the impasse in which a person finds himself concerning his relationship with one or more other people who themselves share this lack

---

5 Excerpts from Chapter 3 of *L'intégration transgénérationnelle*, 2014, Genesis editions, Geneva.

of integration. Through these seemingly meaningless, sometimes banal, behaviors, the *nirvana style* speaks of that which is repressed or denied in the other. These dramas can eventually be played out in real life. In this case, the lack of symbolic transmission becomes responsible for the behavior of the child. The Oedipus myth speaks of none other than this. Secrets, the unspoken, shameful events, unthinkable events, affective dramas, or even lack of dialogue, are among the factors which are a part of these deficiencies in symbolic transmission, which, as we know, have a dramatic influence on succeeding generations.

The behaviors which belong to the *nirvana style* clarify for us particularly well the content of the transgenerational legacies. Didier Dumas[6] explains that "Psychotic children seem to have as their mission the relentless repair of the genealogical past of their family. They are peerless explorers of the trans-generational unconscious. Psychotic children express or relate things which no one can understand. However, when you take them seriously, you perceive what it is that no one understands; in fact, they are exploring the family past which has made them what they are. It is as if they employ the better part of their time roaming in the unconscious of their mother in search of her lost loves: the grandmothers, the grandfathers or the great aunts for whom they, or their mother, were never able to mourn. Autistic children condemn, by their very existence, mendacious silences. They take upon themselves all that which the others can neither think nor say, without anyone in the family realizing it. By their silence, they protect their parents from truths that are

---

[6] Interview with Didier Dumas in *Comment paye-t-on les fautes de ses ancêtres*, de Nina Canault, 1998, Desclée de Brouwer, Paris.

too painful. Psychosis is thus, from this viewpoint, the destiny of a sacrificial descendant, the proof, if one were needed, that what I call familial cannibalism truly does exist. And without an analysis of the genealogy, one cannot understand anything about this radically unconscious dimension of mental devouring." In this same vein of transgenerational influences, concerning psychotic patients whom he has cared for over long periods, Paul-Claude Racamier[7] speaks of the mother's fetishization of her child.

Anne Ancelin-Schützenberger recalls a case presented by Nicolas Abraham, which illustrates precisely this need to embrace a global view of the whole of the existence of a person to make sense of his experience. "Nicolas Abraham (1978) tells the story of a man who knew nothing at all about his grandfather's past. The patient was an amateur geologist. Every Sunday, he would go looking for stones, gather them up, and break them down. He also chased butterflies, caught them and killed them in a jar of cyanide. Up to this point, all of this is quite banal. But the man felt terribly ill at ease and went in search of therapy. He followed several therapeutic regimes, including psychoanalysis - but without any real success. He still did not feel good about the life he was living. But Nicolas Abraham came up with the idea of having the man do some research about his family, going back several generations. The man then discovers that he has a maternal grandfather whom no one talks about! It was a secret. The therapist advises his client to go see the family of his grandfather; whereupon he learns that his grandfather had committed unspeakable acts; he was suspected of having robbed a bank and of probably have done much worse. He had been sent off

---

[7] Paul-Claude Racamier, *Le génie des origines*, 1992, Payot, Paris, p. 59-103.

to "African Battalions" "to break rocks"; and then he was executed in the gas chamber - all of which had been unknown to his grandson. And how did our subject spend his weekends? As an amateur geologist, he went out and broke rocks, and as a butterfly chaser, he caught great butterflies and killed them in a bottle of cyanide. The symbolic circle is closed and it expresses the secret (of the object of his mother), a secret which he did not (even) know."[8]

In this example, the symbolic association between apparently banal activities - geology and butterfly chasing - and the secret history of the grandfather enables us to discover the origin of this man's malaise. Simply taking into account his symptoms was insufficient to help him. We can see that this person speaks about his grandfather through his activities. He is living out a drama which is not his own but which exists *de facto*, in his relationship with his mother, in an inter-individual space. The other in himself is his grandfather. This alienation comes from his mother's failure to integrate her relationship with her father. The transferential necessity which follows is put into action by his son. The son adapts himself to the failings of his mother and keeps alive the relationship to her father which she has not integrated.

The activities of the butterfly chaser and geologist correspond to the *nirvana style*. He renews before the eyes of his mother that which she has failed to integrate. These spontaneous acting outs are attempts to bring to the fore an alienation of which he was unconscious. Transgenerational analysis leads to the discovery of the hidden life of the grandfather, and so enables Nicolas Abraham's client to integrate what

---

[8] Anne Ancelin Schützenberger, *The Ancestor Syndrome Transgenerational Psychotherapy and the Hidden Links in the Family Tree,* 1998, Routledge, New York.

was the source of his alienation in his relationship with his mother.

In this kind of situation, psychoanalytic analysis refers to the absence of a Self. But even if it is not about the Self, the purpose of the behaviors of the *nirvana style* nevertheless are to release the Self which is present in a latent state behind these alienations. So it is more a question of appreciating this condition as an attempt toward emancipation, even if it may appear paradoxical at first glance. The person who behaves in this way, often at the risk of his physical health, is in reality reduced to acting out what he cannot symbolize as inherited failures of integration. As such, the *nirvana style* is a rich language that requires an adequate translation - as is the case with symptoms in general.

The desire which drives the *nirvana style* is not one commonly acknowledged by an individual; even though one cannot, therefore, say that the individual experimenting the *nirvana style* wouldn't have any proper desire. But it concerns another, deeper unconscious relationship which reveals the alienation so that, subsequently, the individual can be recognized as his true Self and not solely as a representative of alienation. This desire testifies a symbiotic bond at the same time as it condemns this imprisonment in the interpersonal space, in an alienating relationship. Nevertheless, the *nirvana style* does cultivate a relationship with the truth. By acting upon the failures of integration, it divulges them and becomes the mirror of the repressed and denied truths which affected the Self.

The "Nirvana principle" refers to an observation of Sigmund Freud[9] concerning a biological or psychological disposition in the form of a tendency towards less excitement. It is a question of a feeling of "oceanic" well-being, a sort of return to the intra-uterine origins.

In my view, the interest of this principle lies in its application to social bonds[10] and not just as a reference to an intrapsychic function. In this way, it becomes possible to understand what leads the Self to assume the "transferential necessity" of someone else: to respond to it comforts the individual who is suffering from an unconscious conflict and lowers the level of excitement experienced upon contact with the other, which corresponds to the *nirvana principle*. In effect, when a transfer occurs, the unconscious conflicts are soothed and the symptoms are diminished, which is beneficial for those around. But, once this kind of transferential relationship is set up, there is no room for the individualization of the desire of the one serving the needs of transferential necessity. He remains the hostage of an alienating relationship. The gratification of a less disturbing relationship that results from the adaptation of the transferential necessity of the other reveals itself to be, in time, a veritable gilded cage.

---

9 Freud saw Nirvâna as an absence of excitement: "One knows that we have recognized in the tendency to reduction, to constancy, to the suppression of the tension of internal excitement, the dominant tendency of the psyche and perhaps of neurological life in general (the nirvana Principle, as Barbara Low put it) as the pleasure principle expresses it." Sigmund Freud, "Au-delà du principe de plaisir", in *Essais de psychanalyse*, 1981, Payot, Paris, p. 104.

10 Thierry Gaillard, "Principe de Nirvâna, transfert et pulsion de mort", in *Ouvertures, articles et clés d'interprétation*, 2012, Ecodition, Geneva, p. 34-55.

In general, when the Self expresses a complex which is non-integrated by others, I propose to say that it is responding to the *principle of nirvana*, which consists of favoring the interpersonal relationship to the detriment of its individualization. Here, it is a principle of reducing excitation whose application, until then limited to the intra-psychic sphere, must be generalized towards the interpersonal bond.

The active aspect of the Self as the recipient of transgenerational legacies is explained by its desire to comfort the other and, perhaps, to gain its love. Most of the time this desire is not recognized, while that which reflects its narcissism is validated by a collective fantasy of individualization which associates it with sublimated desire. In this context, the use of the word "nirvana" attempts to take into account the subordination of the individualized desire in favor of a shared desire, for "us". This situation is best observed in extreme cases, where instead of being able to integrate an event, the adult denies it. Paul-Claude Racamier precisely notes a correspondence between this form of a lack of symbolization and fetishization. "Flirting with depression without being depressed and with delirium without becoming openly delirious, mothers achieve these mental operations like division and denial - which have a very bad reputation for psychological health - without, for all that, presenting the obvious corresponding perturbations. This is because they have succeeded in fetishizing their child. So long as the patient remains in his unbearable position as the fetish incarnate in the eyes of his mother, she will feel intimately reconstituted, but the patient, himself will know the price he pays to spare his mother from living an authentic sentiment of mourning."[11]

---

[11] Paul-Claude Racamier, *Le génie des origines*, 1992, Payot, Paris, p. 63.

This aptitude for taking care of the other illustrates how the *principle of nirvana* functions, as a response to transferential necessity, but also as a cause of alienation. In the case of Oedipus, it is his very "action" of being born which apparently takes care of the problem of the sterility of his parents, without being able to develop as a subject. But Oedipus, responding to the natural need for individualization, defends himself against it, in the unconscious manner of the *nirvana style*, by committing parricide and incest. If the behaviors which belong to the *nirvana style* are susceptible to becoming the object of integration at a later time, that will not be the case for Oedipus until he arrives at Colonus. In the meantime, once the taboos have been revealed, neither he nor anyone else could integrate these events.

The Persona and the Divided Persona[12]

Etymologically, the word "persona" signifies a theatrical mask, as well as the "role attributed to the mask". The mask cultivates the difference between appearances and the more profound reality of the Self. Not only does it separate the impersonal from the authentic, but it also travesties the manifestation of living, that is to say, the movements of the face, to replace it with a fixed appearance, an arrested moment in time, like death. The actor on the stage of the theatre knows that he is another, and the audience thinks likewise. The very definition of the word Persona reflects this contrast as if to remind us all the more that the subject is all that really matters.

---

[12] Excerpts from Chapter 4 of *L'intégration transgénérationnelle*, 2012, Ecodition, Geneva.

With his reference to the Persona, Carl Gustav Jung[13] had already discovered a way of taking into account the influence of the "collective psyche" on each and every one. He presented the Persona as a kind of graft added to the authentic Self, a sign of the construction of a superficial "me" or a false Self. But instead of treating it as a derivation of the collective unconscious, I analyze it more generally in terms of the imposition of an impersonal psyche and alienation. This nuance takes into account the development of the *Persona* not only under the influence of a culture but also thanks to a more specifically familial influence (transgenerational), or even based upon the limited framework of a two-person relationship. The Self/impersonal dyad covers the entire range of possibilities of transfer, in effect, as well as its most intimate operation.

From this standpoint, it appears that each of us is a combination of Self, *Persona* and *nirvana style*. We find ourselves in one of these positions according to our transgenerational legacies, our entourage, our actual circumstances, and our capacity for integration. Consequently, it is not unusual for an individual to behave according to the *nirvana style* in an intimate relationship (reaching out to his mother) even though publicly he would display his *Persona*. It would be up to the Self, with its ability to integrate, to balance its alienations and to work on freeing itself from them.

While the *nirvana style* maintains a truthful relationship to its origins (by how it exposes the origin of its alienations), the division which characterizes the *Persona* distances it from the truth about the Self buried within it. Division is an ambiguous psychoanalytic concept which Freud

---

[13] Carl Gustav Jung, *Dialectique du Moi et de l'inconscient*, 1964, Gallimard, Paris.

presents based on his observation of two antagonistic aspects of the psyche: “Instead of one single psychic attitude, there are two of them; one of them, the normal one, takes into account reality, while the other, under the influence of impulses, detaches the “me” from reality. The two attitudes coexist, but the result depends upon their respective force.”[14] Freud explains the incongruity associated with the division: “Suppose, then, that the “me” of the child finds itself in the service of a powerful desire for revindication which it is accustomed to satisfying, and suddenly it is frightened by an experience which teaches it that the consequences of the continuation of this satisfaction could be a real danger which it would be difficult to bear. [...] The two opposing reactions to the conflict persist as the core of a division of the ego. The process as a whole only seems so strange to us because we assume that the synthesis of the process of the ego takes place as a matter of course. But in this respect, we are obviously mistaken. This synthetic function of the ego, which is of such great importance, has its own particular conditions and takes place in submission to an entire series of perturbations.”[15]

One must, however, recognize the important differences in the nature and the depth of these divisions. Two extreme forms can be distinguished: that which belongs to repression and that which belongs to division. What is repressed is always susceptible to reappear, in the form of symptoms, for example, and it requires putting in place and maintaining resistances. By way of contrast, denial attests to a more radical cut, a symbolization which is much more deficient. Even

[14] Sigmund Freud, *Abrégé de psychanalyse*, 1950, PUF, Paris.
[15] Sigmund Freud, “Le clivage du moi dans le processus de défense”, dans *Résultats, idées, problèmes*, 1992, PUF, Paris, p. 283.

though he really believes he knows something or has perceived it, such a person cannot help seeing something else in it, that is to say, cannot help transferring its psychological need. The functioning of the transgenerational legacies and the degree of alienation which grows in the course of transmission through two generations, can explain this growing difficulty.

When the transgenerational influence is amplified through two generations, it has an even more powerful way of blocking the symbolic functions necessary to integrate the experience of reality. In this way, the failures of assimilation of the first generation favor the establishment of denial in the second generation. The divisions correspond to the amplification of the alienations from one generation to another. These divisions were described by Serge Tisseron, who explains that the unspoken becomes unspeakable in the next generation, and then unthinkable in the third generation.

The most commonly discussed problem of this kind concerns the thematic of sexual differences when, faced with sexual differences, the child denies the absence of the penis among girls and women. The denial of the sexual difference enables the subject to avoid the neurotic conflict which is referred to as "Oedipal"[16]. Transgenerational analysis can explain the lack of integration of the sexual difference with a missing transmission that prevents any development of an operative symbolization of this reality. When understood in this way, the denial, as a manifestation of the psyche's inability to integrate, corresponds to second or third generation transgenerational alienation.

---

[16] The specialized literature will also speak of the economical aspect of castration anxiety with respect to this situation.

The psychological functioning of Laius corresponds precisely to that of the divided Persona. His committing infanticide unmasks the divided Persona of Laius since a neurotic Persona would always remain within the sole repressive discourse - representing the patriarchal authority, *super-ego* like. In reality, the division of Laius is evident throughout the Oedipus myth. Laius himself is the carrier of a good deal of the failures of integration of which one part can be ascribed to transgenerational legacies[17]. He sends them out upon his entourage in the form of divided Personas. It is in this way that he transposes the unaccomplished mourning of the death of his father into the mourning which Pelops experiences with the death of his son Chrysippus.

The Oedipus Complex

The classic psychoanalytic interpretation of the so-called Oedipus conflicts focuses on a problem which manifests during childhood, between the ages of 3 and 5. It is rather common, in effect, to observe new behavior in the child: declarations of love for the parent of the opposite sex (to get married to them), or rivalry towards the parent of the same gender. His demands for love are difficult to satisfy, and his rivalry with the parent of his own gender does not guarantee him better results, on the contrary. But Freud observed that the child loves both parents. That is indeed the heart of his problem. To solve it, the child can re-enact the solution which his parents themselves adopted in their childhood, and which every patriarchal culture encourages. He can learn to repress

[17] From Cadmus to Oedipus, in passing by Polydorus and Laius, the family line of the Labdacids is also marked by difficulties with the legs, asymmetrical legs, leading to claudication, awkwardness, or even swollen feet.

his "incestuous" attachments and postpone the satisfaction of his desire for love to a later time. In return, he identifies himself with the parent of the same sex and wishes to become "like him" or "like her" (if the child does not manage to identify with the person of the same sex, heterosexuality may become a problem). These are complex processes, and repression or denial, transmitted through several generations have a profound effect on those who inherit them. The latter may then make the surprising discovery of the orientation of their desires as if they were due to genetic reality or a random chance.

Even when they are repressed, the "incestuous" Oedipal impulses do not disappear. The original conflict becomes unconscious and displaces its effects within the basic psyche of the child, which transposes the conflict first experienced with its parents into a conflict which has now become internal. The child himself now represses his impulses and keeps them repressed. Freud finds, in this situation a new entity in the psyche of the child, which he calls the "superego". This *superego* is an internalization of the prohibitions which the parents opposed to the Oedipal desires of the child, a sort of graft which is not produced by the child himself, but which comes to him from his entourage.

This *superego* which the child psychologically adopts is an addition or inclusion of the parental discourse in the psyche of the child. "You must..." "You should...", "This is how it is...", are some of the typical *superego* replies to the most insistent questions.

The *superego* is born from the moment it represses the Oedipal impulses. As its source is impersonal, coming from outside the child, it is not the result of an integration. The child simply represses his impulses to "control" the conflicts which they create for him, the way adults do. He plays the adult and, little by little, he gets caught up in his own game to the point that he risks losing his authentic Self. As Freud explains it, in this case, it becomes a question of a "normal" neurosis, which is typical of our modern culture.

In the case of this classic "normal" process of the repression of the Oedipus complex, the external conflict between the parents and the child is thus reenacted internally in the psyche between the *ego* and the *superego*. Freud explains it in these terms. "The repression of the *Oedipus Complex* has not been an easy task. The parents, particularly the father, having been recognized as an obstacle to the realization of the Oedipal desires, the child represses these desires by creating within itself this new entity, the superego, who internalizes this forbidding function of the parents. In a way, it borrows the necessary strength from the father, and this borrowing is an act that has extraordinarily heavy consequences. The *superego* will guard the character of the father; the more powerful the *Oedipus Complex* has been and the more swiftly its repression is accomplished (under the influence of authority, religious instruction, teaching, or readings), the more severely will the *superego* dominate the ego as its moral conscience, or even as the feeling of unconscious guilt."[18]

The Freudian model for the *Oedipus Complex* enables us to understand, for example, the functioning of certain people who blindly apply the rules without taking into account the specific facts of each situation: people who are alienated by an overweening *superego*. When, by way of contrast, the *Oedipus Complex* is integrated, this robotic functioning, "the letter of the law", gives way to the "spirit of the law", which

---

[18] Sigmund Freud, "*Le Moi et le ça*", in *Essais de psychanalyse*, 1981, Payot, Paris, 1981, p. 246-247.

recaptures the original meaning of certain rules and other collective conventions in each new context. This is the essential difference between an impersonal "superego-like" authority and the positive authority of a creature who knows its true Self.

With this kind of "resolution" of the conflict, the Oedipal impulses are kept repressed during the so-called period of "latency", until puberty. When the libidinal forces reassert themselves, for example during puberty or with a trauma, the latent conflict (because it was repressed) comes to the fore again and is capable of producing veritable existential earthquakes. The resistances which have been maintaining the repression up until this point are subject to a harsh test. The most systematic reaction consists of re-establishing the old "solution" by reinforcing the *superego* to keep the repression in place at any cost.

Although puberty is the critical period concerning this return of Oedipal impulses, the repression of the impulses can also be sprung open by such events as passionate love, emotional or traumatic shocks, unexpected events, etc. In any event, as long as the *Oedipus complex* has not been integrated (precisely on account of its repression), it will persist unconsciously. And, like everything that is repressed, it will tend to break through the barrier of the resistances. Even if it does not break through openly, it will serve as the source of various symptoms which are considered "neurotic".

The "Oedipianization" (that is, the structuring of the mind which results from the repression of the oedipal drives) illustrates in an exemplary way the emergence of another in itself, the *superego*, both individually and collectively on a cultural (modern) scale. The conflict with the parents is "solved" in the same way that they resolved it with their own parents. Moreover, Sigmund Freud considered the *superego* of the child as the inheritor of the parental *superego*. In this context, it is possible to consider the repression of the *Oedipus Complex* and the setting up of the *superego* as a sort of alienation, even if it is the alienation of the generalized, collective neurosis.

The edifying function of the parents consists of giving birth to the Self in the child. With parents who, ideally, had already integrated their Oedipal conflicts, the child will have a less intense conflict to deal with, favoring in such a case their integration rather than their repression.

Today, however, a completely different understanding of the Oedipal problem is possible. It stems from the transgenerational interpretation of Sophocles' work on Oedipus. As I have shown in the preceding pages, Oedipus' culpable conduct, parricide and incest, is not the result of the subject's own desire, but rather the expression of his alienation and lack of being a true Self. As Sophocles explains without saying so, the "therapeutic" solution lies in the need to integrate the transgenerational heritages that were at the origin of the Oedipal problem. Legacies that need to be integrated in order for the true Self to develop.

Self-Knowledge

Self-knowledge has to do with the experience of one's true Self. In other words, only the Self can truly have the experience of "knowledge of the Self". It is this part of the individual which functions in relationship to the overall dimension of its own existence "in the here and now". To understand this concept, it is useful to distinguish self-knowledge from abstract and psychological knowledge about the ego, that is, from judgments about itself and information about its person which is perceived as being objective or which claims to be so. Typically, it is the *ego* which believes it knows itself when it refers to the more or less pertinent representations which it creates about itself, or which others make of it. This knowledge "about" the "ego" reflects a kind of positivist and disembodied attitude; ultimately, it is not a matter of knowledge at all, but rather a collection of beliefs about the ego.

Self-knowledge is something quite different: it is an experience of which only the inner Self can partake. It presupposes a direct relationship with the experience of life "in the here and now". In this dimension of the Self, insights operate and are associated with each other anew in the encounter with the perpetual movement of life. Self-knowledge is situated at the level of existence, of *Being* rather than of *Having*. In this position, the Self, self-knowledge and the process of integration are associated in a symbolic dialog with life. That is why the ancient sages insisted upon the importance of knowing one's true Self when they inscribed on the pediment of the temple at Delphi the epitaph: "Know thyself and you shall know the universe and the gods."

Self-knowledge is an omnipresent theme in the Oedipus myth. While he was still the king of Thebes, Oedipus thought he knew himself. But it was only a rational knowledge and not true knowledge. Through the gesture which renders him blind, Oedipus explains that appearances had fooled him and that the power of reason had not reflected the essential truth, *Alètheia* in the Greek.

The discovery of the true identity of his progenitors was also insufficient to transform him into a creature who knew himself. If that discovery enabled the Self in him to be born, it still needed to develop itself. This first step of being born is only the beginning of the work of integration, the journey from Thebes to Colonus. He will have to integrate the whole of his history, and rewrite it, before the discovery about his origins can be transformed into self-knowledge. Once he has arrived at Colonus, he himself will say that he is another, rather than the one who he was. He will also say that his son was born of another, and not of himself. The abandonment of the ego, of any representation of the ego, in favor of the true Self, is what we must understand together with Oedipus when once again he concludes: “It is therefore when I am no longer anything that I become truly human.”

Oedipus will thus complete his rebirth in Colonus. His self-knowledge will have positive repercussions for his guests. Like an initiation into the mysteries of life, Oedipus will bequeath to Theseus a secret that will guarantee his prosperity.

Bibliography

ABRAHAM Nicolas and TOROK Maria (1978), *The Shell and the Kernel*, 1994, University Of Chicago Press.

ATHANASSIOU Cléopâtre, "La lignée de Cadmos" in *Revue Française de psychanalyse, Laïos pédophile: fantasme originaire ?*, tome LVII, april-june, 1993, Paris.

BACHOFEN Johan-Jacob, (1938), *Du règne de la mère au patriarcat*, Editions de l'Aire, 1980, Lausanne.

BALMARY Marie (1979), *L'homme aux statues*, Grasset, Paris.

BONNARD André (1954), *Civilisation Grecque*, tome II, La Guilde du Livre, Lausanne.

CAMPBELL Joseph (1999), *Transformation of Myth Through Time*, Harper Perennia, New York.

CAMPBELL Joseph (2008), *The Hero with a Thousand Faces*, New World Library, Novato, California.

CANAULT Nina (1998), *Comment paye-t-on les fautes de ses ancêtres*, Desclée de Brouwer, Paris.

DELCOURT Marie (1981), *Œdipe ou la légende du conquérant*, Les Belles Lettres, Paris.

DETIENNE Marcel (2006), *Les Maître de Vérité dans la Grèce archaïque*, Librairie Générale Française, Paris.

DEVEREUX Georges, "Why Oedipus killed Laius: a note on the complementary Oedipus complex", *International Journal of psycho-analysis*, 1953, n° 34.

DEVEREUX Georges (1977), *Essais d'ethnopsychiatrie générale*, Gallimard, Paris.

DEVEREUX Georges (1987), *Femme et mythe*, Flammarion, Paris.

DODDS Eric (1959), *The Greeks and the Irrational,* University of California Press, Berkeley.

EURIPIDES, *The Phoenician Women*, 1992, Oxford University Press.

EURIPIDE, *Les Bacchantes* (translated by Jeanne Roux), 1970, Les Belles Lettres, Paris.

EURIPIDE, *Les Bacchantes* (translated by Mario Meunier), 1923, Payot, Paris.

ELIADE Mircea, (1987), *The Sacred and The Profane,* Harcourt Brace Jovanovich.

FINE Alain, "Laïos pédophile et infanticide", in *Revue Française de Psychanalyse*, tome LVII, april-june, 1993, PUF, Paris.

FREUD Sigmund, *Civilization and Its Discontents*, (J. Riviere), 1930, The Hogarth Press.

FREUD Sigmund, *Abrégé de psychanalyse*, 1950, PUF, Paris.

FREUD Sigmund, *Cinq leçons sur la psychanalyse*, 1966, Payot, Paris.

FREUD Sigmund, *L'interprétation des rêves*, 1967, PUF, Paris.

FREUD Sigmund, *Essais de psychanalyse*, 1981, Payot, Paris.

FREUD Sigmund, "Le clivage du moi dans le processus de défense", in *Résultats, idées, problèmes*, 1992, PUF, Paris.

GAILLARD T. Tony, (2020), *Transgenerational Therapy, Healing the Inherited Burden*, Genesis Editions, 2020, Geneva.

GAILLARD T. Tony, (2020), *Shamanism, Ancestors and Transgenerational Therapy*, (collective book), Genesis Editions, Geneva

GAILLARD Thierry (2016), *L'autre Œdipe*, Genesis Editions, Geneva.

GAILLARD Thierry (2014), *L'intégration transgénérationnelle*, Genesis Editions, Geneva.

GAILLARD Thierry (2018), *Sophocle thérapeute*, Genesis Editions, Geneva.

GILLESPIE W.H., "Castration, culpabilité, perversion", in *Les perversions*, 1980, Tchou, Paris.

GOUX Jean-Joseph (1990), *Œdipe philosophe*, Aubier, Paris.

GRIMAL Pierre, (1969), Dictionnaire de la mythologie grecque et romaine, PUF, Paris.

HERMÈS Trismégiste, *Corpus Hermeticum*, tome 1, 2011, Éditions Les Belles Lettres, Paris.

HOMERE, The Illiad.

HUMBERT Jean (1847), *Mythologie grecque et romaine*, Librairie Duprat, Paris.

JUNG Carl-Gustav, *Dialectique du Moi et de l'inconscient*, 1964, Gallimard, Paris.

MÉAUTIS Georges (1957), *Sophocle, essai sur le héros tragique*, Albin Michel, Paris.

MÉAUTIS Georges (1959), *Les dieux de la Grèce et les mystères d'Éleusis*, PUF, Paris.

MUNDER ROSS John, "Oedipus revisited, Laius and the Laius complex", in *Psychoanalytic Studies of the Child*, vol. 37, 1982, Yale University Press.

PETIT Aimé (1991), *Le Roman de Thèbes*, translation in modern french, Champion, Paris.

PLATO, *Complete Works*. Hackett, 1997.

RACAMIER Paul-Claude (1992), *Le génie des origines*, Payot, Paris.

RAND Nicholas, "Psychanalyse du secret dans *Le Fantôme d'Hamlet*" in *Le psychisme à l'épreuve des générations*, under the direction of Serge Tisseron, collected essays, 2000, Dunod, Paris.

RAND Nicholas (2001), *Quelle psychanalyse pour demain ?*, Érès, Paris.

RÉFABERT, Philippe, MÉLÊSE Lucien, DUBARRY Claude and GARNER Georg (1997), *Les Travaux d'Œdipe*, L'Harmattan, Paris.

SCHAEFFER Jacqueline (2000), *Le refus du féminin*, PUF, Paris.

SCHAEFFER Jacqueline, *La différence des sexes dans le couple ou la cocréation du masculin et du féminin*, 2003, Cycle of Introductory Conferences on the Psychoanalysis of the Adult, published at www.spp.asso.fr

SCHÜTZENBERGER Anne Ancelin (1998), *The Ancestor Syndrome: Transgenerational Psychotherapy and the Hidden Links in the Family Tree*, Routledge, New York.

SOPHOCLE, *Tragédies*, 1973, Gallimard, Paris.

SOPHOCLES, *The Three Theban Plays*, translated by Robert Fagle, Penguin Classics, 1984, New York.

STATIUS Publius Papinius, in D. R. Shackleton Bailey (ed. and trans.), Statius 2: Thebaid Books 1-7. Cambridge, Mass.: Harvard University Press, 2003.

SZONDI Peter, (2002), *An Essay on the Tragic*, Stanford University Press.

TISSERON Serge (1995), *Le psychisme à l'épreuve des générations : clinique du fantôme*, Dunod, Paris.

TISSERON Serge, "Les secrets de famille, la honte. Leurs images et leurs objets" in *La psychanalyse avec Nicolas Abraham et Maria Torok*, collective essays under the direction of J.-C. Rouchy, 2001, Éres, Paris.

VELIKOVSKY Immanuel (1969), *Oedipus and Akhenaton,* Doubleday, New York.

VERNANT Jean-Pierre et VIDAL-NAQUET Pierre (1994), *Œdipe et ses mythes*, Complexe, Bruxelles.

VERNANT Jean-Pierre (1990), *L'univers, les dieux, les hommes*, Seuil, Paris.

VIAN Francis (1963), *Les origines de Thèbes, Cadmos et les Spartes*, Librairie Klincksieck, Paris.

www.ingramcontent.com/pod-product-compliance
Ingram Content Group UK Ltd.
Pitfield, Milton Keynes, MK11 3LW, UK
UKHW022001190726
13853UKWH00004B/1654

9 782940 540358